AF247588

Life of the People

Realist Prints and Drawings from the Ben and Beatrice Goldstein Collection, 1912-1948

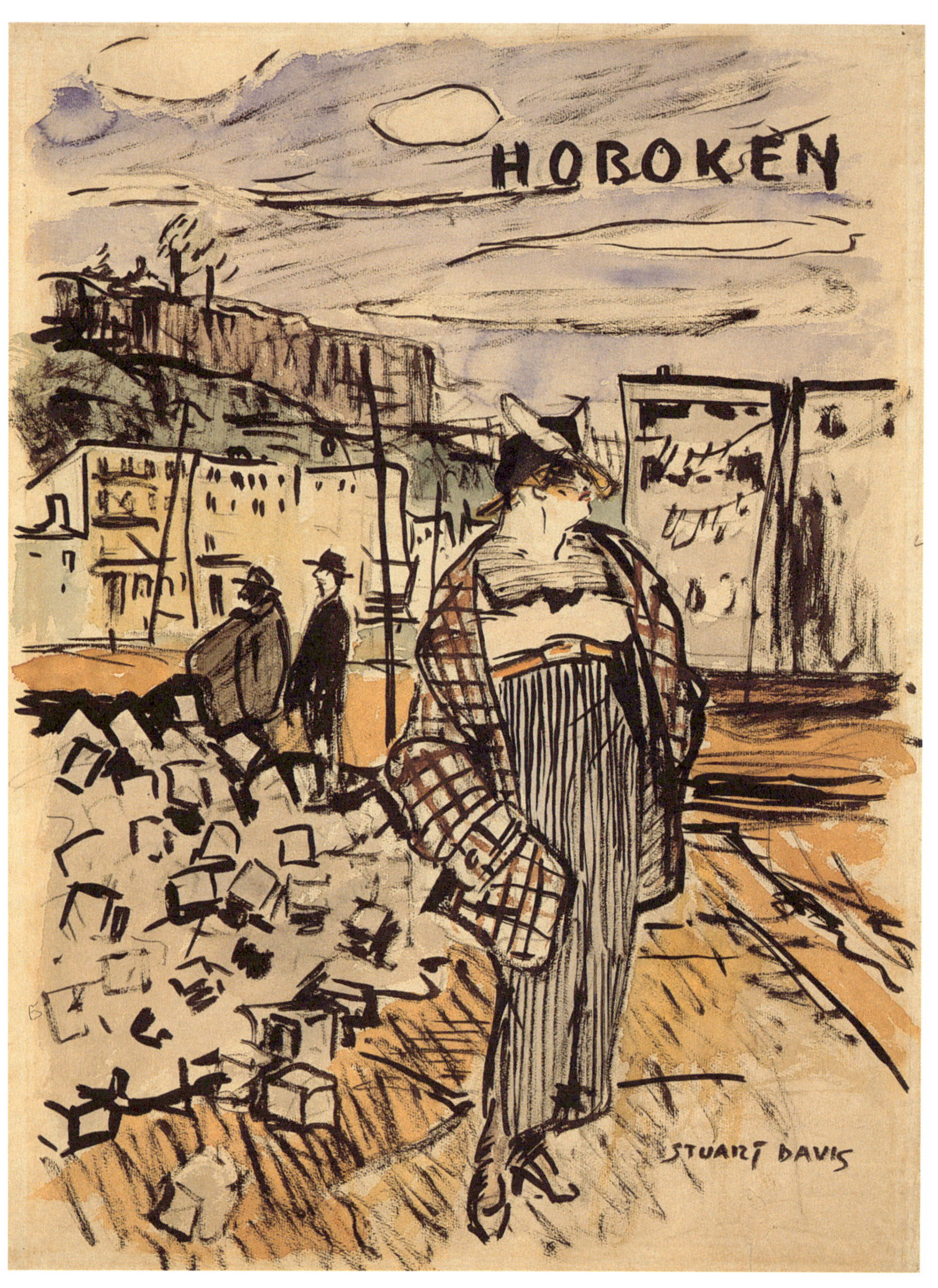

HOBOKEN
STUART DAVIS

Life of the People

Realist Prints and Drawings from the Ben and Beatrice Goldstein Collection, 1912-1948

edited by HARRY L. KATZ

with essays by Bernard F. Reilly, Jr., and Garnett McCoy

Washington

Library of Congress

1999

Figure 1
STUART DAVIS. *Hoboken.*
Watercolor. 1916.
Copyright © Estate of Stuart Davis /
Licensed by VAGA, New York, N.Y.

Stuart Davis's watercolor drawing was published in 1918 in the *Liberator*, whose editor, Max Eastman, described Hoboken as "a city about a square mile, over in the smoke across the Hudson, shuffling down the beginnings of the Palisades to the edge of the water with a loose collection of factories and railroad yards and cheap flats." Of Davis's style, Eastman wrote that "His art lives among the same squalid and strong-smelling and left-out objects, and it goes its sordid way with the same suave dirty muscular self-adequate gracefulness of power."

An exhibition at the Library of Congress, October 20, 1999-January 29, 2000

This publication was made possible by a generous contribution from the Ben and Beatrice Goldstein Foundation. The exhibition received support from the Alfred and Elizabeth Bendiner Memorial Trust and the Caroline and Erwin Swann Memorial Fund for Caricature and Cartoon.

Library of Congress Cataloging-in-Publication Data
Life of the people : realist prints and drawings from the Ben and
   Beatrice Goldstein collection, 1912–1948 / edited by Harry L. Katz
   with essays by Bernard F. Reilly and Garnett McCoy.
       p. cm.
    Exhibition catalog.
    Includes bibliographical references and index.
    ISBN 0-8444-0993-6 (alk. paper)
    ——— Z663.39 .L54   1999
    1. Prints, American Exhibitions. 2.—20th century—United
States—Exhibitions. 3. Prints, Mexican Exhibitions.
4. Prints—20th century—Mexico—Exhibitions. 5. Politics in art
Exhibitions. 6. Goldstein, Ben, 1909–1995—Art collections
Exhibitions. 7. Goldstein, Beatrice—Art collections Exhibitions.
8. Prints—Private collections—United States Exhibitions.
9. Prints—Washington (D.C.) Exhibitions. 10. Library of Congress.
Prints and Photographs Division Exhibitions.   I. Katz, Harry L.
II. Reilly, Bernard.   III. McCoy, Garnett.   IV. Library of Congress.
NE508.L52   1999
769.973'074'753—dc21   99–31621
                                                           CIP

Front cover: *Miner Joe,* 1940, by Elizabeth Olds (pl. 4). Reproduction courtesy of the Estate of Elizabeth Olds.
Back cover: *Hoboken,* 1916, by Stuart Davis (fig. 1). Copyright © Estate of Stuart Davis /
Licensed by VAGA, New York, N.Y.

Contents

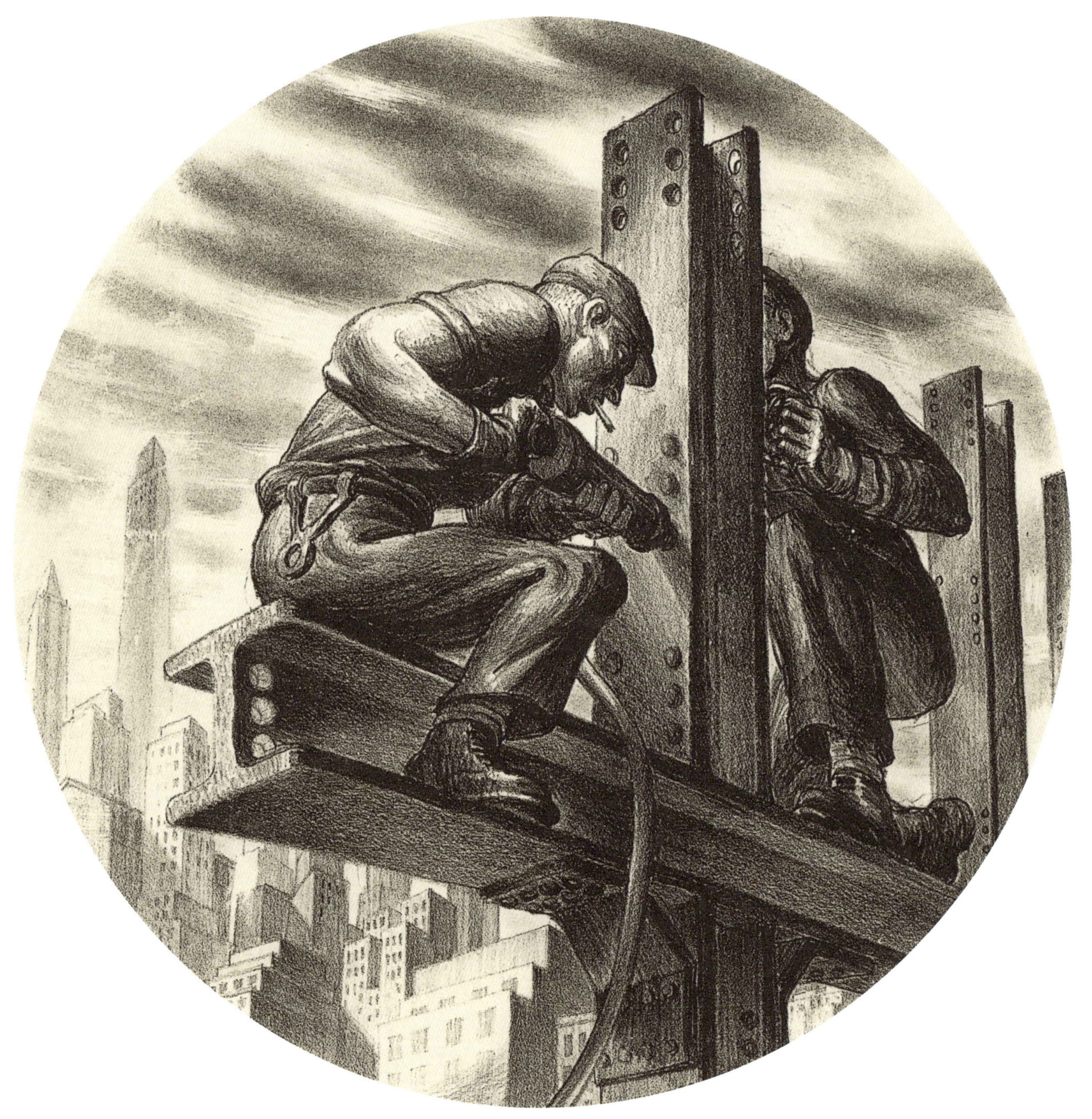

Figure 2
HARRY STERNBERG. *Builders.*
Lithograph. 1935-36.

Harry Sternberg, who was born and grew up on the Lower East Side of Manhattan, influenced generations of American realist artists and pioneered the artistic development of commercial print processes such as screenprinting and offset lithography through his activities with the Works Progress Administration (WPA) Graphics Division as well as by teaching graphic arts at the Art Students League in New York City from 1933 to 1968. He worked for the Federal Art Project in 1935-36.

In 1993, the Ben and Beatrice Goldstein Collection arrived at the Library of Congress. Acquired in part as a purchase, the remarkable collection comes to the Library primarily as a magnanimous gift that is being donated to the nation over a period of twelve years. Ben Goldstein (1909-1995), a native New Yorker, a labor advocate, and a garment manufacturer, amassed an extraordinary gathering of drawings and prints over several decades. With the active support of his wife Beatrice, he put together a collection of artworks that reflected his interest in the city of his birth, the American people, and the human condition. Picturing the life of this people over the course of the first half of the twentieth century, some two thousand prints and drawings spanning the years 1900 to 1950 form the heart of the collection. Another sixteen hundred works include posters relating to social protests dating from the 1960s and 1970s, portfolios of Mexican and American prints and illustrations, and eighteenth- and nineteenth-century English and American political satires from *Puck*, *Judge*, and *Harper's Weekly*. Out of the core collection of two thousand prints and drawings, we have selected for the current exhibition fifty-nine works from the United States and Mexico, dating from 1912 to 1948. These tumultuous years saw two world wars and the Great Depression and witnessed an unprecedented level of political and social activism among American artists.

Ben Goldstein believed that his collection had found an appropriate home at the Library of Congress, an institution whose holdings span the full range of intellectual and creative achievement in this country and include materials representing many other cultures around the world. The Goldstein Collection joins the holdings of the Prints and Photographs Division, which include graphic art as documents of social and political commentary as well as representations of creative endeavor. Here is found the largest collection of American political prints and drawings in existence, including works by many of the most influential graphic artists of each generation. Works by such European masters as Goya, Gillray, Daumier, Grosz, and Kollwitz, as well as the largest surviving collection of printing blocks by Jose Guadalupe Posada, the influential Mexican popular printmaker, provide a rich setting for the Goldstein Collection.

As shown in *Life of the People* and the exhibition it documents, Goldstein's collection depicts the American scene, representing a broad spectrum of social and political issues concerning labor and industry, life in urban centers, work and play in rural areas, and the experience and achievements of minority groups. Urban and industrial themes coexist with images of the land, suggesting connections between working people of all types, from builders and miners to soldiers, farmers, or office girls. The prints and drawings in the exhibition were created during a period of intense political and social activism on the part of artists, beginning just before World War I and ending after World War II. This exhibition highlights in particular images from the 1930s, when the turmoil and uncertainty of the Depression led increasing numbers of artists to turn toward social concerns for their subject matter. It includes a number of landmark images in the history of American political art, an important example being Robert Minor's iconic drawing entitled *Pittsburgh* (fig 8). But it also presents humorous, light-hearted depictions of life in the early twentieth century as well, such as Martin Lewis's *Boss of the Block* (fig. 14) and Mabel Dwight's *The Clinch, Movie Theatre* (pl. 7).

Comprising notable works by major artistic figures such as Stuart Davis, John Sloan, George Bellows, Thomas Hart Benton, and Isabel Bishop, the Goldstein Collection also includes the work of less well-known but gifted artists such as Blanche Grambs, Joseph Hirsch, Elizabeth Olds, and Prentiss Taylor. It embraces not only the work of women artists but also African American and Mexican artists who shared Ben Goldstein's concerns. The collection represents the legacy of realist artists Robert Henri, John Sloan, and Thomas Hart Benton, under whom many of the artists in the exhibition studied and who stood as advocates of representational art. These realist artists rejected abstraction—in spite of its growing influence in America—as irrelevant and inaccessible to the people. The "American Scene" printmakers such as George Bellows, Mabel Dwight, and Hugo Gellert—named for this subject matter—often blurred the line between fine and popular art. They took their medium—usually lithography—their simplified style, and their ironic look at daily life from the cartoons and illustrations in popular periodicals.

Artists at this time argued that prints should be a product for the many. New concepts in the production, marketing, and reproduction of original works of art offered the public access to an entire generation's artistic output and promoted the relevance of fine art to everyday life.

This new democratization in art was epitomized by the resurgence in the use of lithography as an artistic medium. Particularly in the prints made by artists employed by the Federal Art Project of the Works Progress Administration, we see the transmutation of the silkscreen from commercial use to its use in fine art for the production

Figure 3
THOMAS HART BENTON. *Goin' Home.*
Lithograph. 1937.
Copyright © T. H. Benton and R. P. Benton Testamentary Trusts / Licensed by VAGA, New York, N.Y.

Seeking to gain a broader audience for his work, Thomas Hart Benton, best known as a muralist and leader of the Regionalist movement in American art, created a number of lithographs based on his drawings, paintings, and murals. He commented on this lithograph: "From a drawing made 1928—in North Carolina Smokey Mountain country. With a companion driving the car I followed these mill people till the drawing was finished."

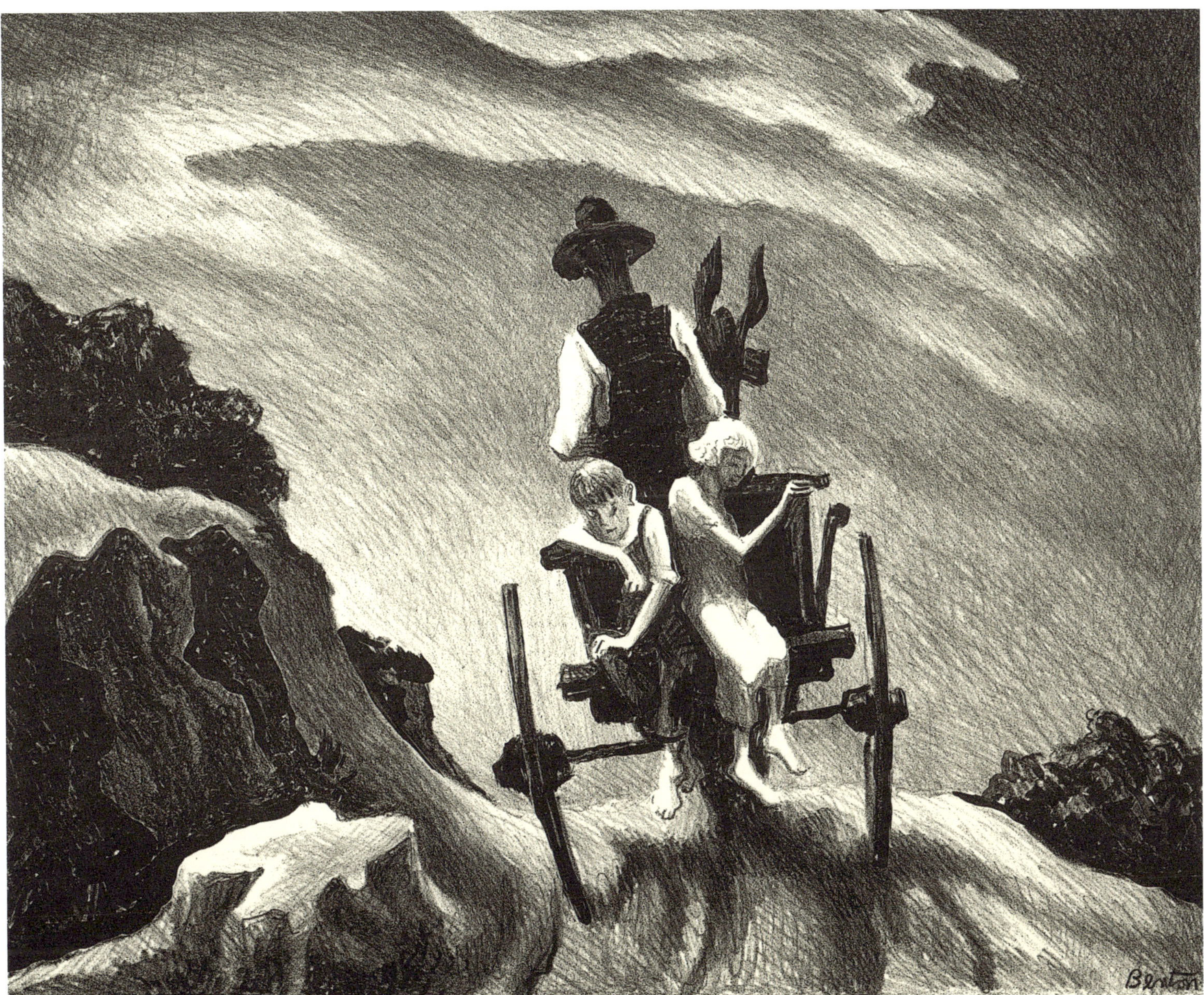

Benton

of large, colorful, and inexpensive editions, making artistic images of ordinary working people affordable and widely available.

It is this "art for the people" that appealed to Ben Goldstein. All of us at the Library of Congress are indebted to the Goldstein family—especially to Ben, Beatrice, Elinor, and Joel—as well as to William and Kathy Brody for their generous support, encouragement, and assistance. We are grateful to Bernard F. Reilly, Jr., former head of the Curatorial Section of the Prints and Photographs Division, for his efforts in bringing the Goldstein Collection to the Library of Congress and for his appreciation of Ben

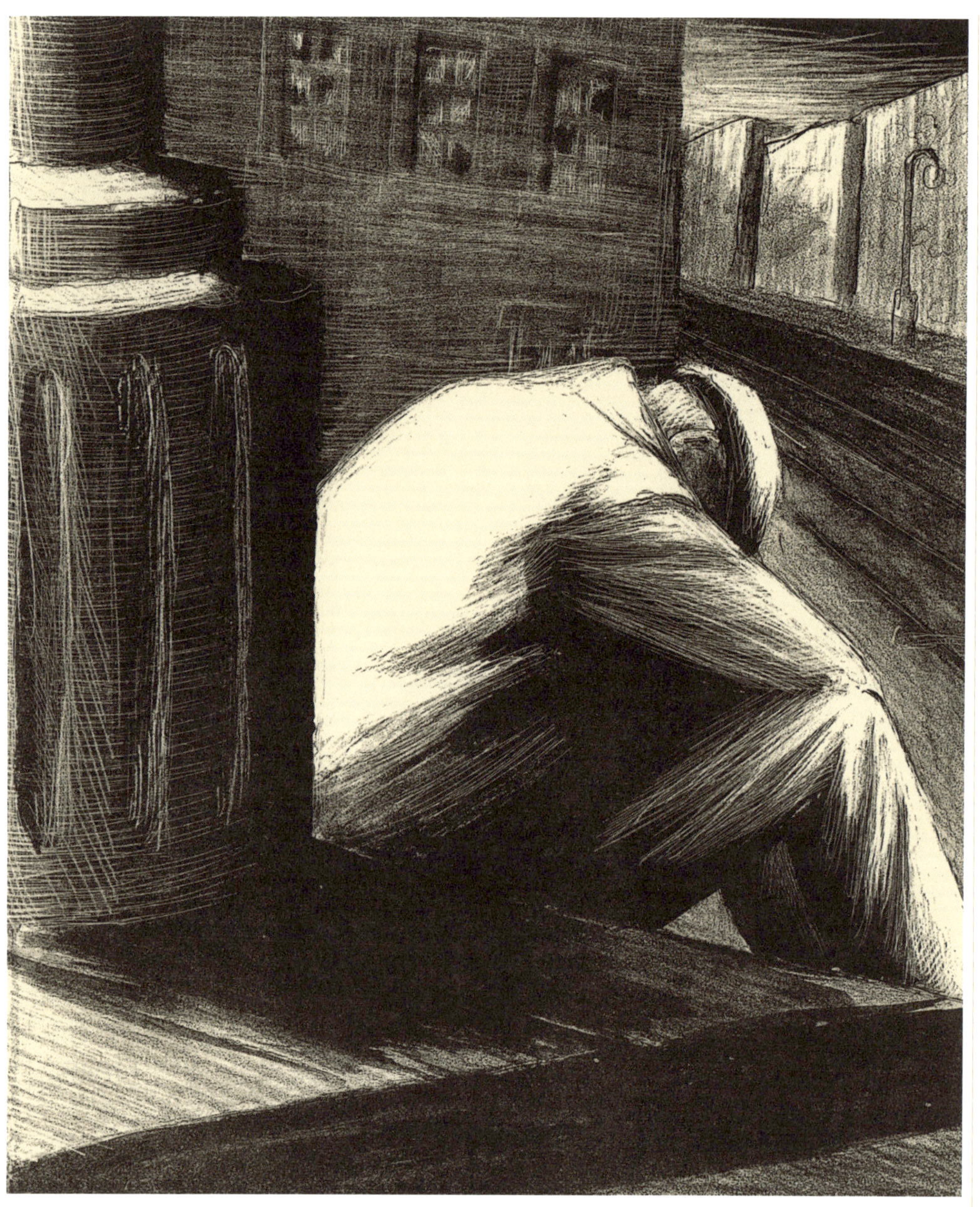

Figure 4
BLANCHE GRAMBS. *No Work.*
Lithograph. 1935.
Reproduction courtesy of
Blanche Mary Grambs.

The defeated figure portrayed in *No Work* by Blanche Grambs exhibits the emphasis her teacher Harry Sternberg placed on the depiction of the rawness of life in the Depression and gives visible form to her interest in Marxist economics, which she studied at the New Workers School.

Goldstein in this volume. Besides benefiting from the help of Ben and Beatrice Goldstein themselves, Bernie enjoyed the assistance of James Fraser, Fairleigh Dickinson University; William Brody, Lawrenceville, New Jersey; and the artist Charles Keller. We thank Garnett McCoy, Curator Emeritus and former Editor at the Archives of American Art, for his insightful essay that enhances our understanding of this period in our history. We are grateful to Sara Duke, Curatorial Project Assistant, for writing the captions and notes on the artists, with the help of many artists, curators, and others, including the following: Karol Lawson, Columbus Museum, Columbus, Georgia; Robert Ellis; Laura Muessig, Frederick R. Weisman Art Museum, University of Minnesota; Elizabeth G. Seaton; Sender Garland, Boulder, Colorado; Erika Gottfried, Tamiment Library, New York University; Susan Teller, Susan Teller Gallery; Priscilla Haile, Sumter Gallery of Art, Sumter, South Carolina; Paul Buhle, Brown University;

Patricia Lynagh and the staff of the National Museum of American Art/National Portrait Gallery Library; Linda McCurdy, Rare Book, Manuscript, and Special Collections Library, Duke University; Alison Gallup, VAGA; and Nicole Acarino, Vanderbilt Fine Arts Gallery.

At the Library of Congress, thanks for their contributions to this publication go to Ralph Eubanks, Director of Publishing, Evelyn Sinclair, Editor, and Gloria Baskerville-Holmes, Production Manager, Publishing Office. For their contributions to the exhibition, we are grateful to Irene Chambers, Director, Interpretive Programs Officer; Giulia Adelfio, Exhibition Director; Deborah Durbeck, Production Officer; and Chris O'Connor, Production Specialist, all in the Interpretive Programs Office. Other Library staff members who assisted in this publication and exhibition were Elena Millie, Maricia Battle, Katherine Blood, Lisa Lee, Noah Bardach, and

Woody Woodis of the Prints and Photographs Division; Harold Boyd of the Loan Division; Lynn Brooks, Domenic Sergi, and Michael Smallwood of Information Technology Services; Jim Higgins and Yusel El Amin of the Photoduplication Service; and Holly Krueger and Anne Fuhrman of the Conservation Office.

And, finally, Harry Katz, Curator of Popular and Applied Graphic Arts, Prints and Photographs Division, has our sustained gratitude for shepherding this project from the beginning. The Library of Congress also wishes to acknowledge the Alfred and Elizabeth Bendiner Memorial Trust Fund and the Caroline and Erwin Swann Memorial Fund for Caricature and Cartoon for their support of this exhibition and publication.

Linda Ayres
Chief, Prints and Photographs Division
1997-99

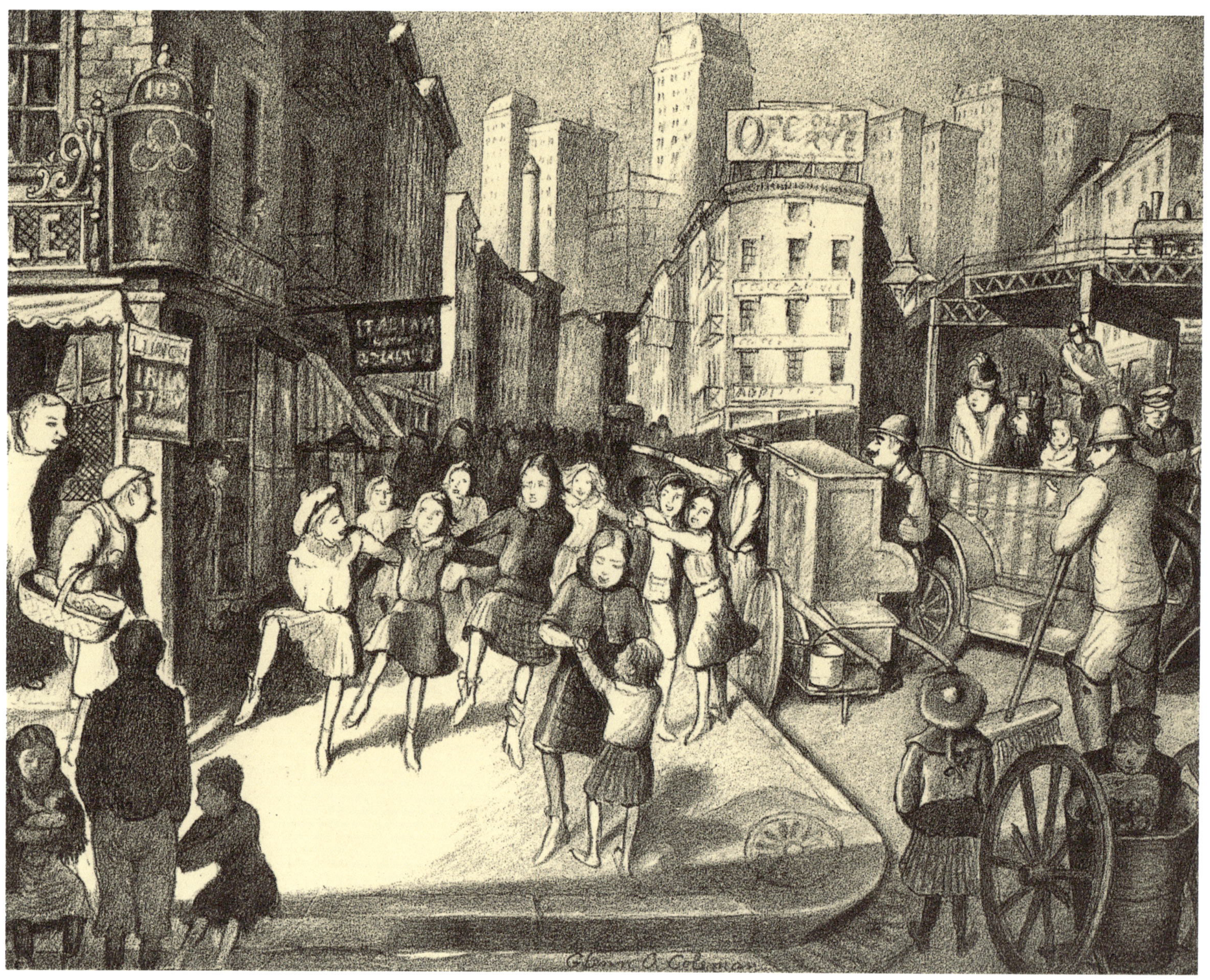

Ben Goldstein: His Legacy   Bernard F. Reilly, Jr.

Ben Goldstein left to the Library of Congress—and to the nation—a collection of prints, drawings, and paintings informed, as very few art collections have been, by a sympathy for the condition of working people. Neither the collection nor the gesture is surprising for one who spent most of his life absorbed by the politics and economics of human toil.

Ben Goldstein's affiliation with art and with the world of American labor politics began almost simultaneously. Born in New York in 1909, Ben came of age in the city at the beginning of the Great Depression. The scarcity of jobs there led him to retreat up the Hudson River to Westchester County to the resort areas of the Hudson Highlands, where he found work as a waiter and busboy. There he met members of an older generation of artists and writers of the political left and formed what would become lasting friendships with them. Around 1910 the town of Croton-on-Hudson had become a rural retreat for such figures from the cultural and political avant garde as writer Mabel Dodge, dancer Elizabeth Duncan (sister of Isadora), and, briefly, the journalist John Reed. Later, during the early 1930s, Croton's Mount Airy section became a haven for American radical artists and writers Max Eastman, Robert Minor, and Boardman Robinson, William Gropper, and Anton Refregier, who sought refuge there from the reaction against American radicalism that followed the First World War. Here Ben Goldstein bonded to both the people and the environment. In the late 1930s he bought a house in Croton, where he and his wife Beatrice, or Bea, lived and raised their family, making it their home until 1962.

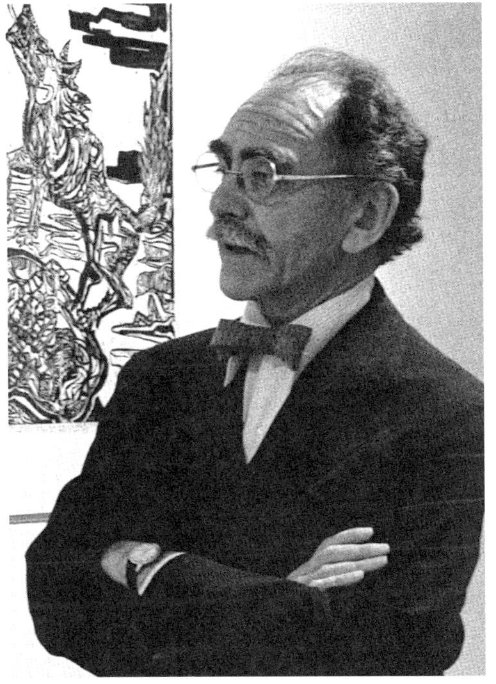

Figure 5
GLENN O. COLEMAN.
Hurdy Gurdy Ballet. Lithograph. 1928.

Glenn O. Coleman studied under Robert Henri and, like his classmate George Bellows, focused his artistic energy on scenes observed from life in the streets of New York. Although his oil paintings are relatively unpopulated, Coleman's lithographs teem with the city's inhabitants and, like *Hurdy Gurdy Ballet*, explode with urban energy and vitality.

Figure 6
Ben Goldstein (1909-1995).

Whether through a natural inclination toward the left or because he was influenced by the political ideology of his Croton associates, Ben plunged into the midst of the New Deal's campaign to reshape American labor-capital relations. In 1933, he worked on Fiorello LaGuardia's mayoral campaign. Then he served as labor adviser on the garment industry to FDR's short-lived but influential National Recovery Administration until the agency was declared unconstitutional and dissolved in 1935. At this juncture, Ben began to study industrial engineering with particular emphasis on the analysis of time and motion. From 1936 to 1942 he worked in the garment industry under the collective bargaining agreement, helping unions and manufacturers scientifically determine piece-work production quotas. Ben also served as an impartial chairman, adjudicating disputes between manufacturers and needle trade unions such as the International Ladies' Garment Workers' Union (ILGWU).

After World War II Ben continued his association with the garment industry, but henceforth as a manufacturer rather than a labor advocate. He bought a small loft factory on Sixteenth Street in New York, and for the next fifteen years or so ran this operation providing women's sportswear for the wholesale and retail trade.

Ben prospered at this endeavor and began to buy art in earnest. Earlier he had acquired a number of drawings and prints from Robert Minor, Hugo Gellert, and other artists of the political scene and from various artists employed by the Works Progress Administration. Many of Ben's purchases, at this time and later, were a form of financial aid to artists in need. But a steady and substantial income from the factory now allowed him to step up his collecting activity. Ben later recalled that he would spend his mornings reading the newspaper ("I was more concerned with the state of the world than with art!") and directing business at the factory. In the afternoons he combed the galleries on Tenth Street and elsewhere in lower and midtown Manhattan for prints and drawings about working people, American industry, politics, and other subjects that few other collectors found desirable.

In his collecting Ben took the artists of *The Masses* as a point of departure. From these latter-day artists he was gradually drawn backward to nineteenth-century political artists like Thomas Nast and Daumier and, even further back in time, to Hogarth and the anonymous satirists of the French Revolution. He also looked forward, acquiring work by Mexican artists of the Taller de Gráfica Popular, and even by such artists of the postwar period as Oliver Harrington, David Levine, and Sue Coe.

Whatever the historical period, Ben maintained that what interested him was "art that related to life." He objected to

Figure 7
ADOLF DEHN. *Central Park at Night.*
Lithograph. 1934.
Reproduction courtesy of the
Estate of Adolf Dehn.

Adolf Dehn left his native Minnesota for New York City in 1917 and ultimately settled there after years of intermittent travel. Of *Central Park at Night*, the artist said, "My lithographic problem was to try to get the velvet blacks of the foreground, the intense glow of light and the dull glow of the sky with the skyscrapers towering, and yet marching across the format of my paper. This I tried to do by combining pure washes with rubbed tones, scratching and scraping these down to light grays and pure whites, and then drawing strong blacks over the rubbed and washed tones."

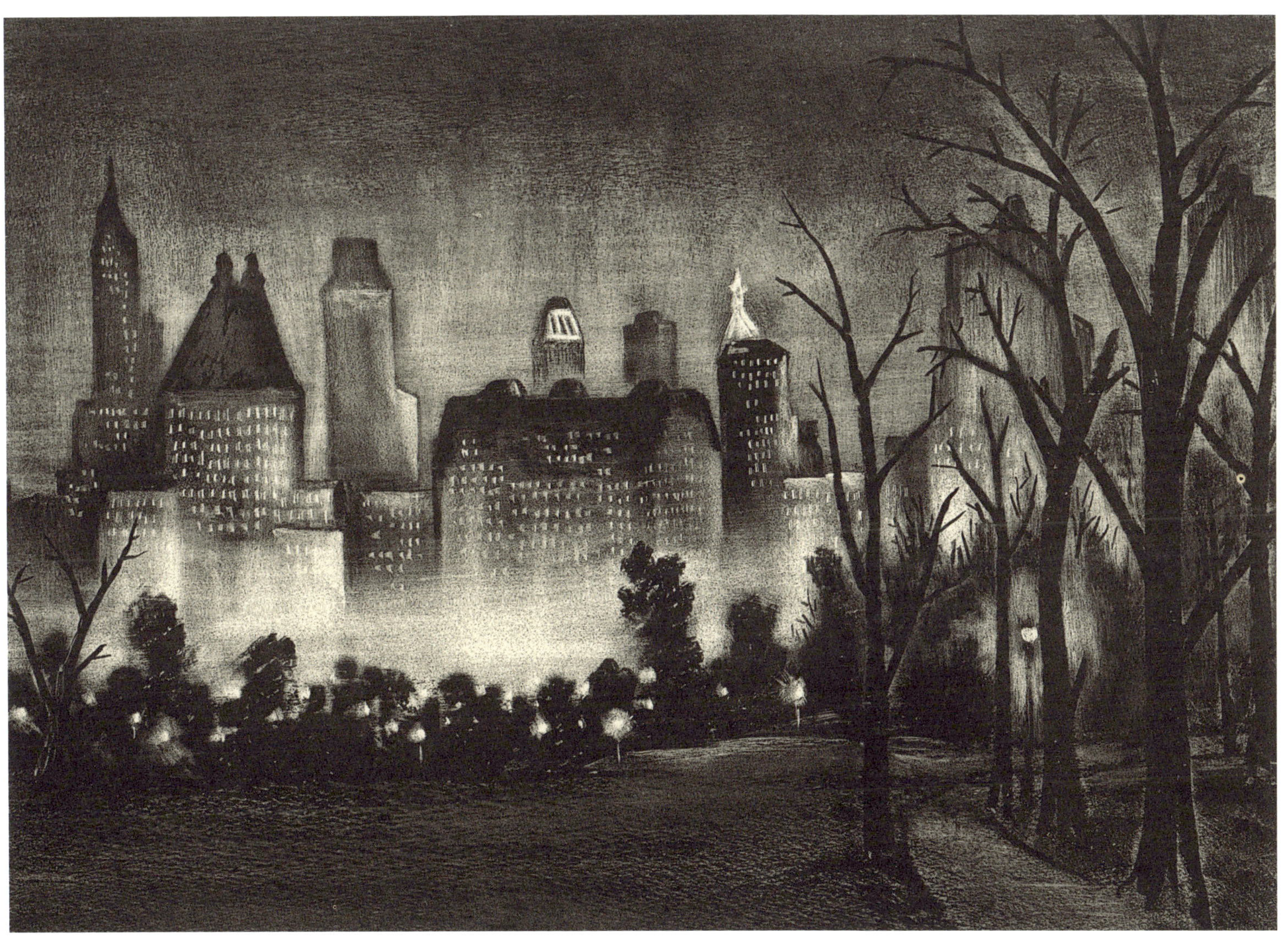

abstract art, which he claimed was "not about anything." Such antimodernist ideas were in the wind even in the early 1950s. A comparable argument-on-principle against abstract art was advanced by the aging Ben Shahn in his book *The Shape of Content* (Cambridge: Harvard University Press, 1957). Underlying the thinking of both Ben Shahn and Ben Goldstein was the peculiarly modern liberal notion of art as a receptacle and transmitter of enduring human social values. This view posited a role for artists as social critics, upholding such values or ideals as nonviolence, individual liberty, and intellectual freedom in the face of hostile forces prevailing in their respective societies. Shahn and others saw a noble ancestry of artistic idealism stretching back to early modern artists like Goya, Jacques Callot, Daumier, Rembrandt, and others.

Ben's holdings rapidly increased and he quickly ran out of room for the collection in his small apartment on East Nineteenth Street. He began to display his collection pieces on the walls of the factory. The exhibit became something of a sensation and attracted to the loft a steady stream of interested curators, scholars, and collectors from across the United States and abroad. What drew these visitors was the novelty of what was by then a substantial art collection devoted to social and political themes. One suspects, though, that some of Ben's visitors were as intrigued by the sight of the very real exertions of stitching and cutting by nearby garment workers mirroring the toil of their pictorial counterparts in the "socially conscious" art on the walls above them.

Ben often recounted the story of a burglary of his unlikely art gallery. One night during the mid-1960s intruders broke in and made off with adding machine, typewriters, television set, business equipment, cash, and even the staplers from the loft, but left all of the art on the walls.

Ben's collecting soon became more methodical and ambitious. In 1969 a professor friend at Lincoln University in western Pennsylvania confided to Ben his frustration at not being able to find materials to illustrate his lectures on black history. Intrigued, Ben set about gathering together from artists, galleries, and various other quarters prints and drawings on the subject of African American life in America. These he assembled in a highly popular exhibition for the college entitled *The Black Experience*.

In New York Ben persuaded Pratt Graphics Center director Fritz Eichenberg, himself an artist and a contributor to *The Nation,* to let him create an expanded version of the exhibition at the center. For this undertaking Ben enlisted the help of historian Philip Foner and the African American artist Romare Bearden. Again the exhibit was tremendously successful, and for ten years it traveled to various universities and museums across the United States.

Ben had found his mission: he saw his collection as a lesson in history, and himself as instructor. There followed a succession of exhibits based on the Goldstein collection. For each exhibit, Ben would seize upon an issue or a concept, such as war, presidential scandals, or women as artists and then would collect works that addressed that theme. Around his chosen theme Ben would weave a web of stories or lessons, historical anecdotes with a sprinkling of liberal mythology, in the form of introductory essay and captions.

In 1972 with James Fraser he mounted *Up against the Wall,* an exhibition on political graphics, at the New York Cultural Center. Subtitled "Protest Posters from Three Centuries," the exhibit in fact included broadsides, lithographs, and woodcuts—as well as posters—dating from the American Revolution to 1972. It included the work of modern artists such as Romare Bearden, Käthe Kollwitz, Steinlen, Stuart Davis, Hugo Gellert, Ben Shahn, Faith Ringgold, and many of their anonymous forebears. The exhibition had tremendous resonance for a generation of students, artists, and even curators who had grown up during the fractious days of the 1960s student revolts and who embraced the idea of art as a form of activism.

In 1976, at the age of sixty-eight, Ben sold the loft and closed his factory. In his decision he cited the changing nature of the neighborhood. What art Ben couldn't store in his apartment went into a storage vault in lower Manhattan. From the vault, selected pieces would occasionally emerge for the exhibits that Ben continued to do well into his eighties. Eventually Ben and his wife Bea came to believe that their long-standing desire to share the works in the collection would be best served by placing them in a public institution. Some of these works they donated to the New York Public Library. But the majority of the collection Ben and Beatrice Goldstein placed in the Library of Congress, to be held by the nation's library.

The collection, more than most assemblages of works of art, embodies a message. Its individual pieces speak, stridently at times, of political struggle, of the travails of working people, and of the urban industrial experience. But the message of the Ben and Beatrice Goldstein Collection as a whole is far richer and more nuanced than any of its parts. It is about the enduring dignity of all people across the economic and national spectrum. As Ben was fond of saying about his art, "It's important." This importance becomes more and more clear as the collection is viewed, used, and studied by succeeding generations.

Life of the People   Garnett McCoy

I have been collecting and searching for graphic art (drawings-lithos-etchings-etc) that relate to social, political, and ethnic issues. I started from "The Masses" (1911-1917), then to "the Liberator" (1918-1924), "The New Masses" (monthly 1926-1932), and "The New Masses Weekly" (1934-1940 so far). These are the most important American artists that include Henri, Glackens, Sloan, A. B. Davies, Bellows, Higgins, B. Robinson, Mahonri Young, Glintenkamp, Stuart Davis, Art Young, Bob Minor, etc. . . . The point I am making is that the great artists related to the social and economic issues of their day.

Ben Goldstein to Rockwell Kent,
September 19, 1969[1]

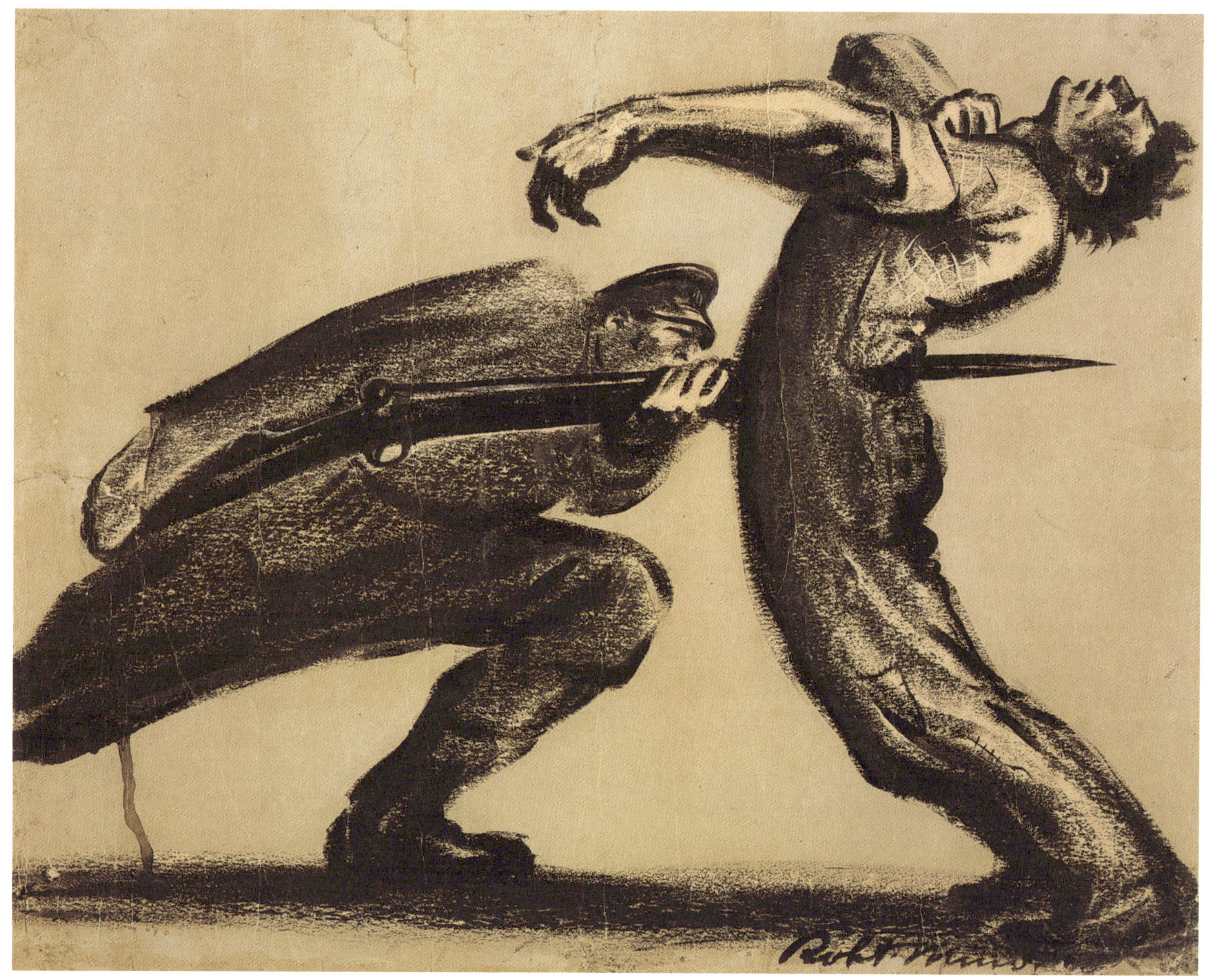

With startling impact, Robert Minor's drawing *Pittsburgh* called attention to the use of weapons against unarmed workers striking against the United States Steel Corporation in the summer of 1916. Minor's image is a potent visual attack aimed at one incident among hundreds of strikes between 1890 and 1920 where federal or state troops or armed guards intervened, invariably on the side of the employer. In Pittsburgh, the Coal and Iron Guards, an official Pennsylvania state police force established in 1894 to break strikes, was called to the plant, where they fired "round after round from riot guns into the crowds of men, women, and children who were calling to their fellow workers to come out from industrial slavery and be free industrial men." What the workers wanted was an eight-hour workday. The article reporting on this event in the socialist magazine *The Masses* in July 1916 stated that the attack "killed five workers and wounded sixty others."

A Texan who worked as a newspaper cartoonist in San Antonio and St. Louis before settling in New York in 1912, Robert Minor began contributing drawings to *The Masses* in 1915. The strength and character of his work, inspired in part by his passion for Honoré Daumier and in part by his own militant radicalism, comes through in Minor's protest against this common practice in labor disputes, targeting the large corporations' routine hiring of armed guards, who often acted with brutal dispatch in the event of conflict. In its simple yet dynamic design, Minor's picture (published in August) illustrating the earlier article in *The Masses* on the shooting of workers near Pittsburgh is a moving expression of outrage, of protest, and of solidarity. In some ways it typifies the prints and drawings from the period between 1912 and 1948 that Ben Goldstein admired, sought out, and collected.

A sense of change and a spirit of rebellion both figured prominently in the American art world in the early twentieth century. Some of the best—and best known—artists in New York contributed to *The Masses*, among them John Sloan, the young Stuart Davis, a youthful Glenn Coleman, George Bellows, Robert Henri, and Boardman Robinson. Minor joined the editorial board in 1916. Even the ethereal Arthur B. Davies published illustrations in the magazine during its heyday. Like much of the work produced by the developing urban realist movement, art appearing in *The Masses* during this

Figure 8
ROBERT MINOR. *Pittsburgh.*
Lithographic crayon and India ink. 1916.

Born in Texas, Robert Minor revolutionized editorial cartooning in the years before World War I by introducing new media—crayon and ink brush—to a field dominated by pen-and-ink drawings. His liberating technical innovation, derived from the work of such European masters as Francisco Goya and Honoré Daumier, enabled him to create spare, forceful drawings, including his masterpiece of gestural drawing, *Pittsburgh,* which he drew for *The Masses* during a 1916 steel workers' strike.

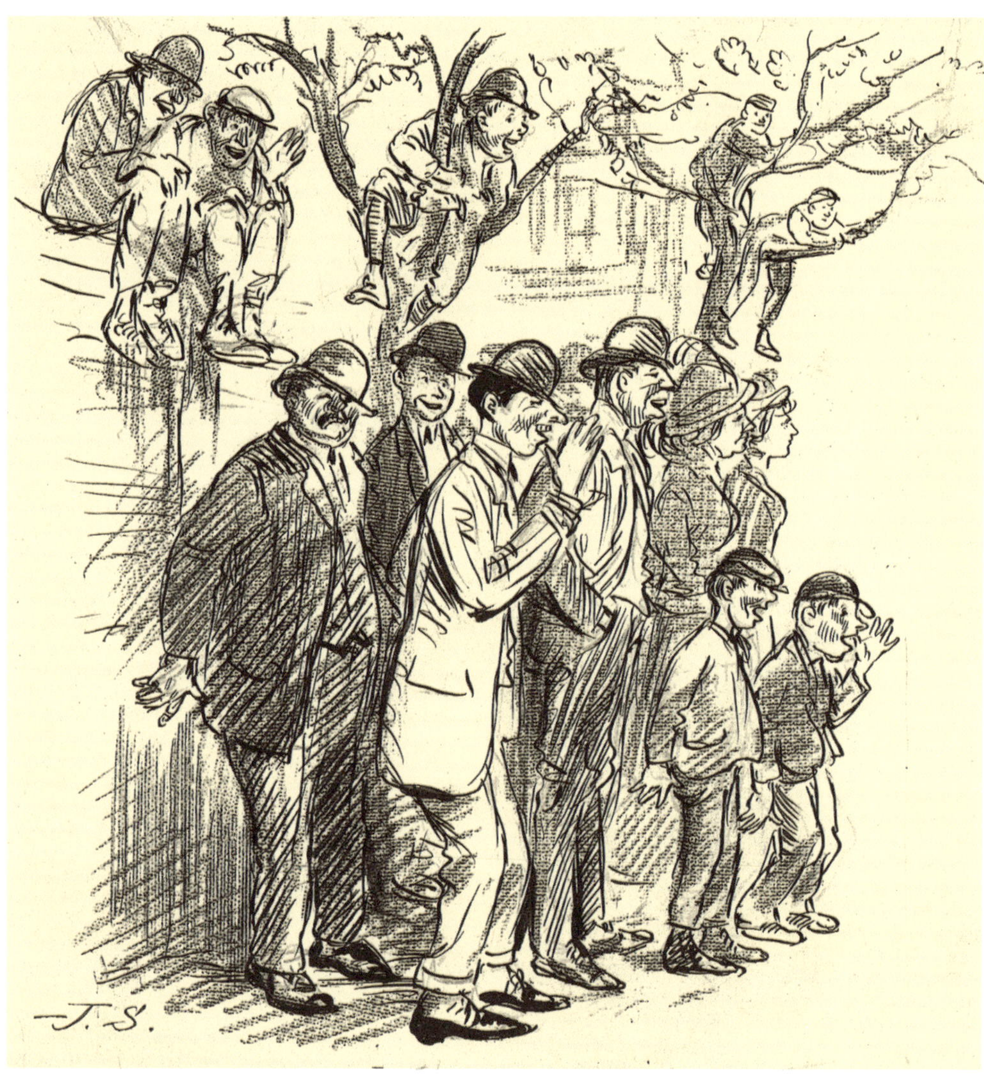

JOHN SLOAN.

"Tee Hee" Boys: Born with a Vote and a Partial Sense of the Ridiculous.
Ink and crayon. 1912.
Reproduction courtesy of
the Estate of John Sloan.

John Sloan began his career as a newspaper sketch artist and made his name as a member of the circle of young American artists that formed around Robert Henri, becoming known as the New York Realists or the Ashcan School. To supplement his income, Sloan drew illustrations for mainstream magazines like _Collier's_ and _Century,_ as well as for such radical leftist journals as _The Call_ and _The Masses._ This acerbic caricature of antisuffrage males jeering a suffragette parade in New York City on May 4, 1912, appeared in _Collier's._ Insightful observation, a keen sense of humor and irony, a reforming spirit, and an easy realist style are hallmarks of Sloan's illustrative work.

Figure 10

GEORGE BELLOWS. _In the Subway._
Lithograph. 1921.
Reproduction courtesy of Mrs. Earl M. Booth.

George Bellows imbibed the realist teachings of Robert Henri and John Sloan as a student in New York. Between 1921 and 1924 he collaborated with master printer Bolton Brown on more than a hundred images, including _In the Subway,_ and spurred new interest in lithography as a fine art medium.

period from 1912 to 1917 depicted with sympathy, but without sentimentality, the life of ordinary people. Much of it was sharply and wittily satirical at the expense of corporate control, religious authority and hypocrisy, and increasingly, military power. City living was a constant theme.

Social and political issues began to get full play in magazines after the turn of the century. A women's suffrage parade in New York on May 4, 1912, marching from Washington Square to Carnegie Hall to ask for the vote, provoked John Sloan's *"Tee Hee" Boys*, satirizing a common male reaction to the event when it appeared in *Collier's Weekly* two weeks later. The Triangle Shirtwaist Company fire that killed 146 women when it broke out on the ninth and tenth floors of the garment factory just before quitting time on March 25, 1911, received Henry Glintenkamp's bitter comment in *Girls Wanted* (pl. 2), done in lithographic crayon and published in *The Masses* in 1916 when an investigative report finally came out. Glintenkamp's drawing seems to echo the spirit of the memorial procession of 200,000 people that marched in utter silence ten days after this tragedy of American labor history. In *Hoboken* (fig. 1), published in the *Liberator* in 1918, Stuart

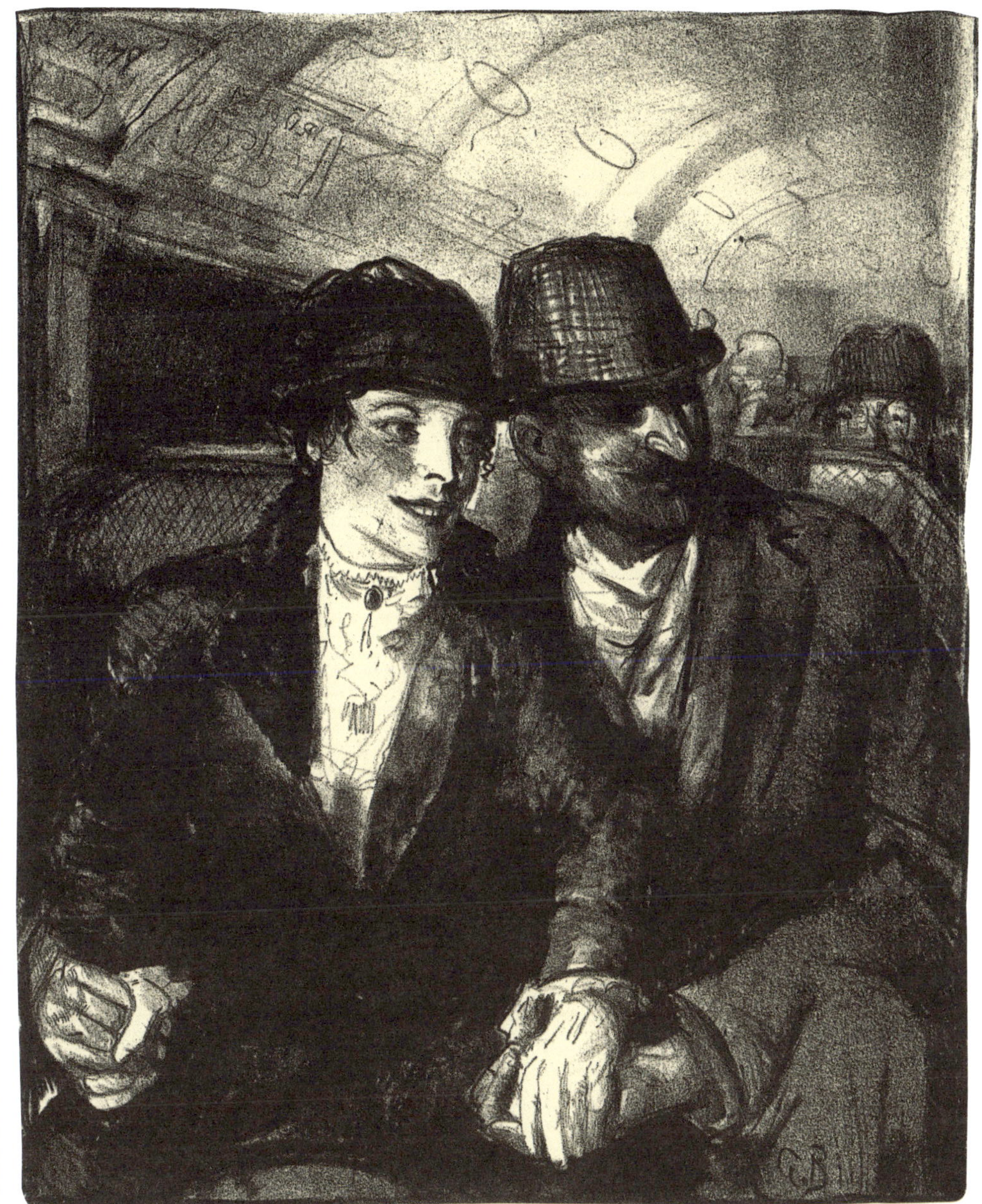

Davis, who shared studios with Coleman and Glintenkamp, celebrated his favorite town outside New York City. Davis's sardonic cartoons or drawings turned up in almost every issue of *The Masses* between 1913 and 1916.

Years of shattering social and economic disruption on a worldwide scale are recorded in pictures collected by Ben and Beatrice Goldstein that recall this often-neglected aspect of early twentieth-century history. Between 1905 and 1912 major revolutions broke out in Russia, China, and

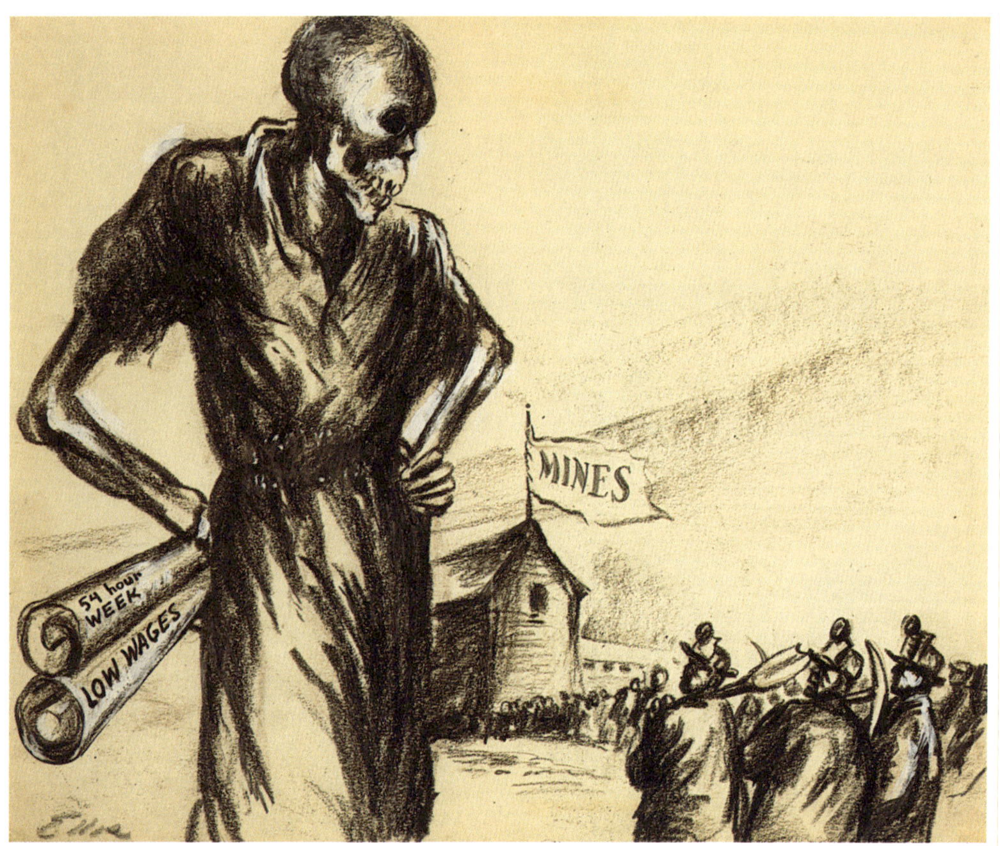

Figure 11
FRED ELLIS. *54 Hour Week / Low Wages.*
Crayon, ink, pencil, and opaque white.
Ca. 1930s.
Reproduction courtesy of Robert Ellis.

Political cartoonist Fred Ellis learned his craft from Robert Minor and shared his mentor's concern for the plight of the working man, a concern that is apparent in *54 Hour Week / Low Wages*, which shows death as the reward for long hours with little pay for miners.

Figure 12
PEGGY BACON. *Heywood Broun.*
Lithograph. 1930.
Reproduction courtesy of
the Estate of Peggy Bacon.

In the fall of 1930 Bacon dashed off her satirical image of the journalist Heywood Broun for an American Printmakers exhibition. This picture of Broun at his typewriter was subsequently published in *Off with Their Heads!* (1934), with her description: "…Sits in black leather chair with floppily crossed feet in god-awful mess of letters and litter. Looks like a stage elephant made of two men. Mild, journalistic anxiety stamped on face. Must-get-the-article-in look."

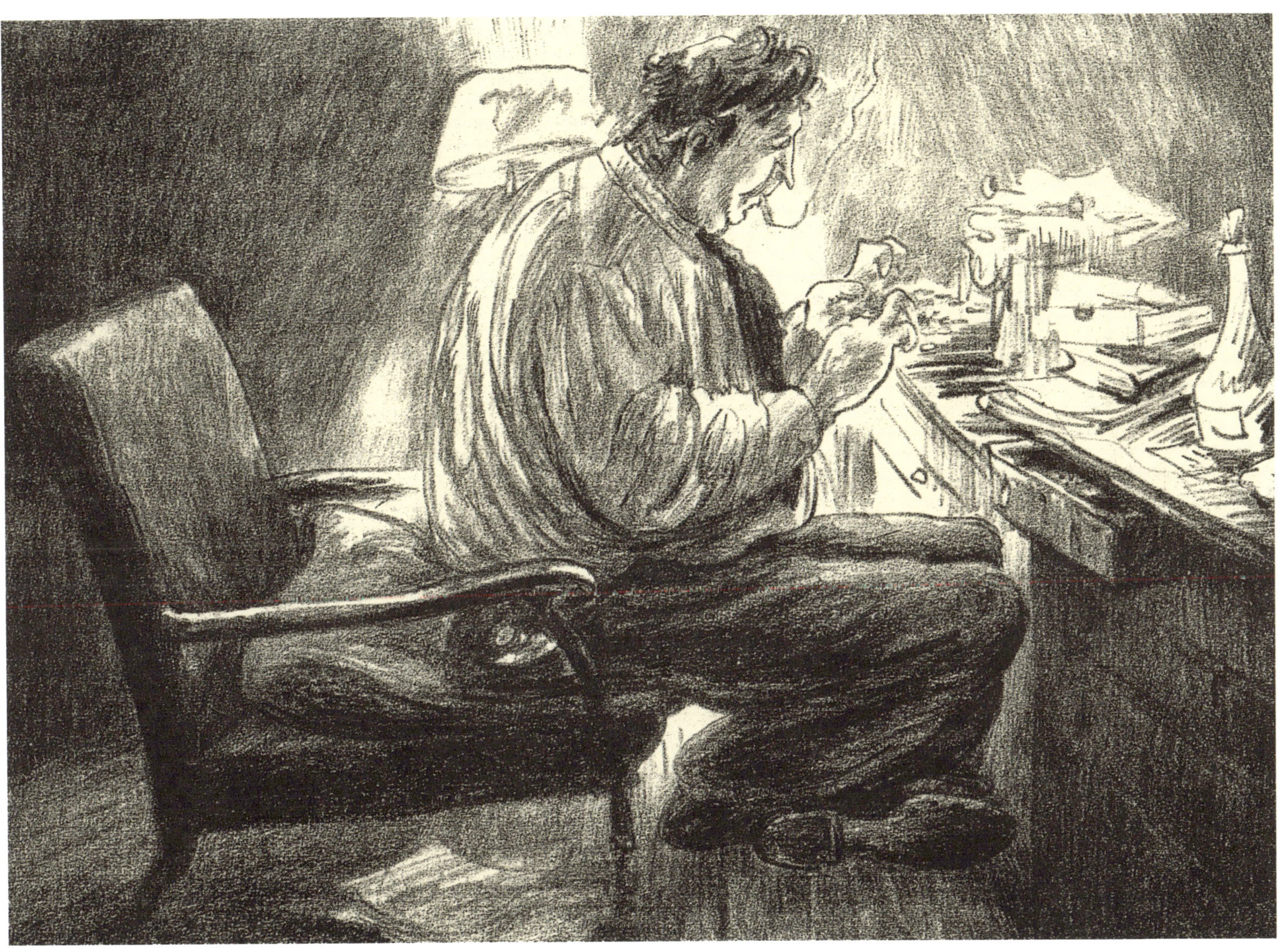

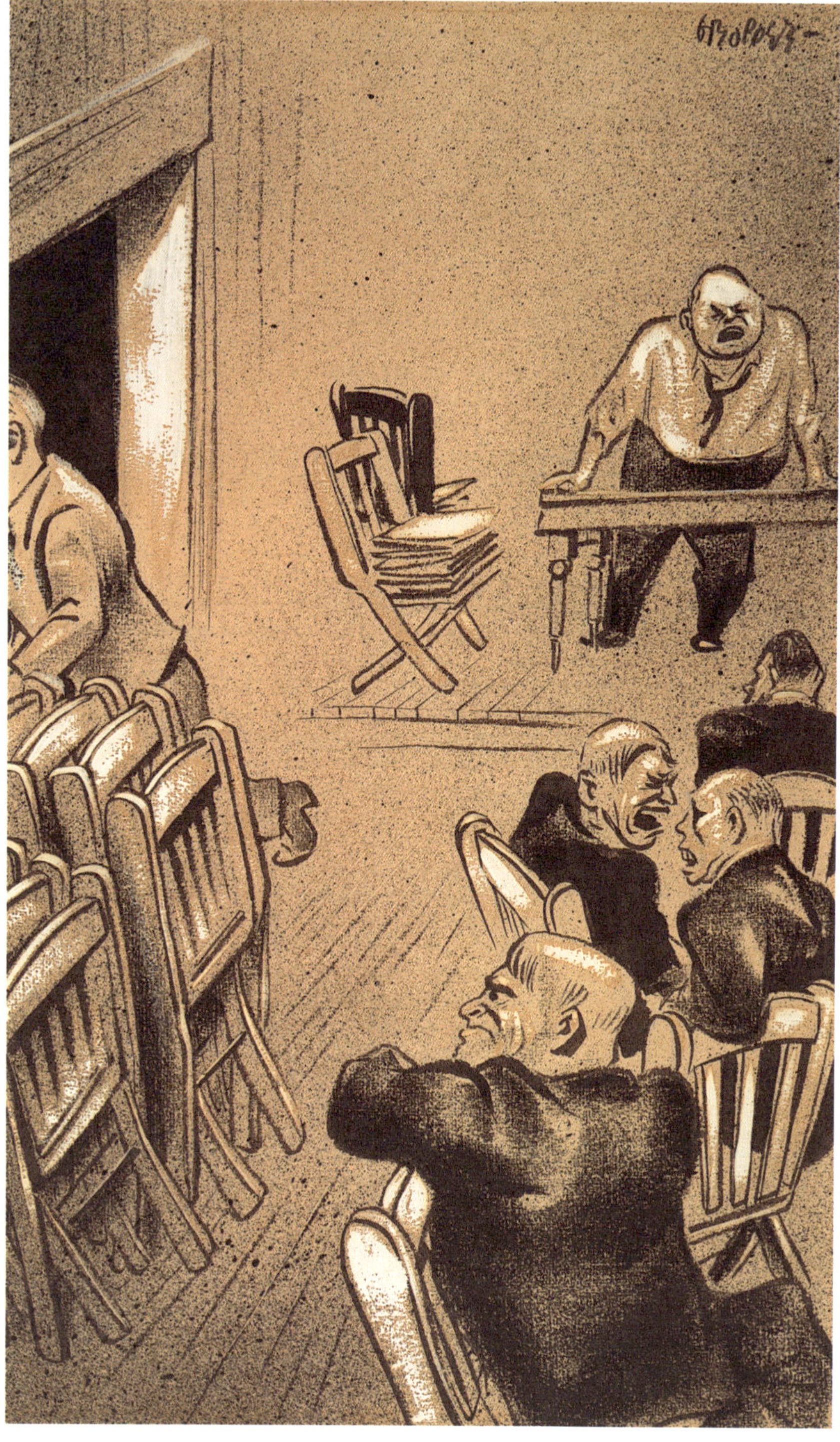

Figure 13
WILLIAM GROPPER.
The Troublemaker Who Acts Like a Provocateur at the Caucus.
Ink and white with spatter. 1943.
Reproduction courtesy of Gene Gropper.

His early studies with Robert Henri and George Bellows gave William Gropper, the son of poor Jewish immigrants to New York's Lower East Side, the artistic tools to express graphically his passionate commitment to the social and economic welfare of the working classes. This image appears among Gropper's illustrations for the novel *Abreml Broide* by Ben Gold, published in Hebrew in New York in 1944.

Mexico. Increasingly militant expressions of popular discontent took place in Persia, Turkey, Egypt, Portugal, and the Balkans. World War I spawned the Bolshevik revolution of 1917, which established the Soviet Union, inspired less successful upheavals in Germany and Hungary, and unleashed nationalist agitation in much of the colonial world. Nor did the United States escape the turmoil and ferment of the time. At the turn of the century, vast and profound change rent the fabric of American society.

From the closing of the frontier in 1890

through the continuing waves of immigration, disclosures of corrupt business control of government at all levels, and massacres of strikers and their families by National Guard troops or by private armies, an increasingly strong sense of popular discontent arose in the United States. Until the outbreak of World War I and the development of the internal combustion machine gave new impetus to the American economy, doubts began to surface about the viability of capitalism itself. In 1912 Eugene Debs, Socialist Party candidate for president, got nearly a million votes, more than double the number he had received four years earlier. In 1913 more than two hundred socialist newspapers and journals were published in cities and towns across the nation. The weekly *Appeal to Reason*, published in Girard, Kansas, had a circulation of 760,000 that same year. Garment and textile workers' strikes in and around New York City, occasionally crushed with appalling violence, impelled intellectuals, middle class reformers, and even bohemian artists and writers to offer support to the labor movement.

As the nation's economy entered a period of fundamental change, so did its culture. A new wave of young artists in New York who sought to break free from the grip of conventional academic painting found a leader in the charismatic artist and teacher Robert Henri, who spoke glowingly of Walt Whitman, the eloquent anarchist Emma Goldman, and Leo Tolstoy. He insisted that art must reflect life. Henri inspired a promising school of realists—including John Sloan, George Bellows, and Glenn Coleman (fig. 5). Henri and Bellows taught art classes at the Ferrer Center, an anarchist school, and Sloan, a committed socialist, served on the editorial board of *The Masses* for several years.

Pictures meant to arouse protest, expose hypocrisy, and engage sympathy were not the only ones favored by young rebellious artists of the time. Drawings and prints appealing to a common humanity found a growing audience open to change from hackneyed conventions in illustration. "Drawing is a human language, or way of communicating between human beings," John Sloan said. "What the artist does with a piece of charcoal [is] to make lines and tones that define and describe realities seen with the heart and mind."[2] Max Eastman, editor of *The Masses* from 1912 to 1917, spoke of drawing as a means of mass communication: "Drawing is destined to a high place among the arts for drawing, like music, can be adequately reproduced and widely distributed. And while this has appeared a detriment in the light of aristocratic ideals, in the light of democracy it is a fine virtue. The ideal of democracy has indeed given to many artists of our day a new interest in drawing."[3]

Robert Minor himself emphasized the innovative character of spontaneity and directness. "There has been a change in the newspaper field lately," he wrote in 1912. "Newspapers are becoming more sincere. It is but natural that cartoons should become direct, less superficial, less 'stylish,' more natural." "Of course," he added, "there is more of art in the new way."[4]

In America the radical impulse of the prewar years declined sharply after 1918. The Russian revolution split the socialist movement into two warring camps, each of them further weakened by internal factionalism. Political repression following American entry into World War I and culminating in the xenophobic Palmer raids of 1919 and 1920 had an intimidating effect. Prosperity on the one hand and a quiescent labor leadership on the other dampened militant demands. Most of the nation's socialist publications died off. At the same time, a promising "art for the people" movement died out with the collapse of the People's Art Guild, an organization that exhibited contemporary paintings and sculpture in settlement houses, churches, and union halls.

As the market for American impressionism and the milder expressions of modernism boomed in the 1920s, satirical graphic work of a political nature declined in popularity. Some of the best cartoonists of the earlier years—notably Sloan, Boardman Robinson, and Maurice Becker—abandoned

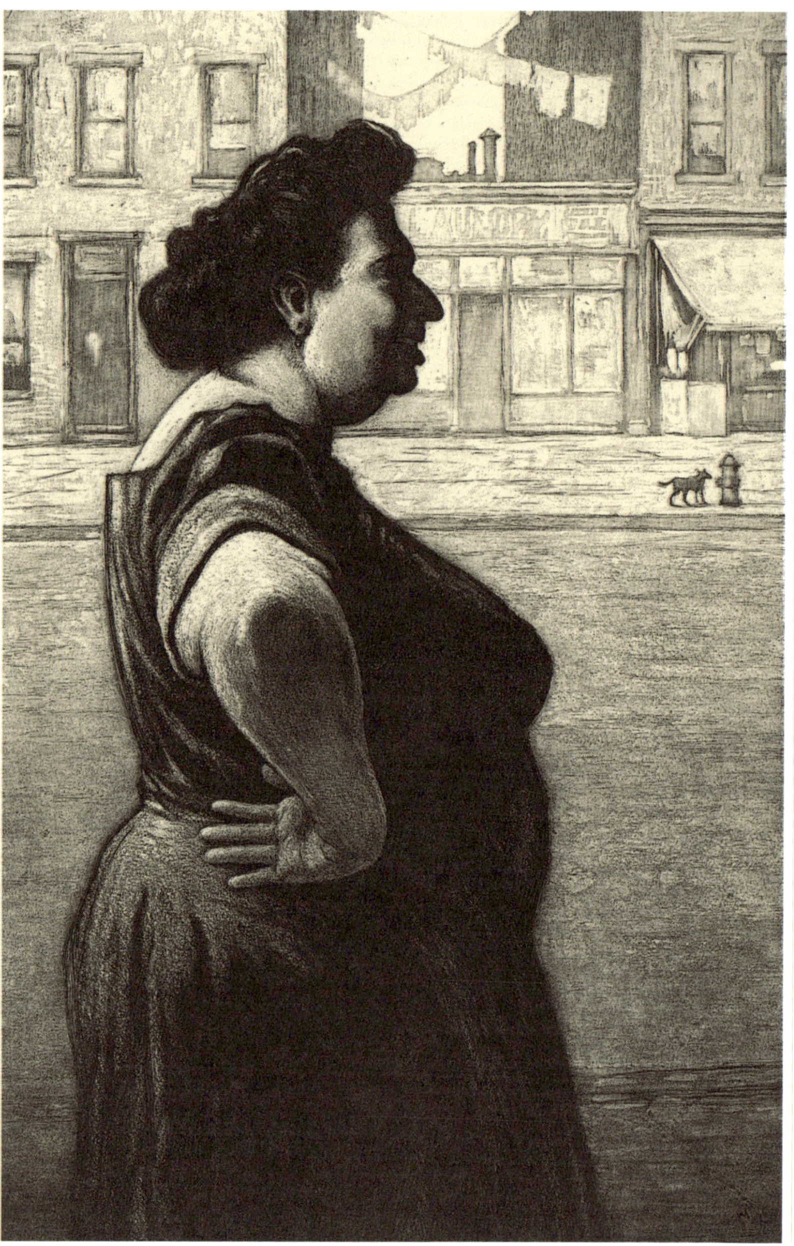

Figure 14
MARTIN LEWIS. *Boss of the Block.*
Aquatint and etching. Ca. 1939.
Reproduction courtesy of
the Estate of Martin Lewis.

Martin Lewis imbued New York City, its skyscrapers, streetscapes, and citizens, with a rare elegance through his technical mastery of such traditional fine art intaglio print processes as etching, drypoint, aquatint, and mezzotint. He chose to work independently during the Depression, rather than participating in the Federal Art Project, and produced few prints between 1936 and 1939. Those that he did create during the period, however, like *Boss of the Block*, are among his most memorable works.

the form to concentrate on painting. Robert Minor gave up art altogether to become a full-time Communist Party writer and functionary. Under the seemingly permanent good health of the economy, the set of values promoted by Henri and *The Masses* lost much of its audience.

Even so, a distinct continuity of protest art can be traced throughout the entire first half of the century. When *The Masses* was suppressed by the government for its anti-war stance in late 1917, it was succeeded by the *Liberator*, whose editorial board and contributors initially included many of the same artists and writers. Some fresh talent came aboard, most notably William Gropper, Louis Lozowick, and the poet and illustrator Lydia Gibson, who married Robert Minor in 1922. After the *Liberator* died in 1924, another attempt to maintain the old tradition was made two years later with the founding of the *New Masses*. The *New Masses* drifted into the Communist orbit as the party's chief cultural publication, carrying sharp satirical cartoons and decorative drawings by Gropper, Lozowick, Hugo Gellert, Peggy Bacon, Adolf Dehn, Glenn Coleman, and Reginald Marsh.

If the early years of the century had been unsettled, the turmoil of the 1930s made them seem in comparison almost a time of placid contentment. A catastrophic crisis followed the stock market collapse of October 1929, and the rapid unraveling of the entire economy renewed, more forcefully than before, questions about whether capitalism was a desirable or even a practicable system. Throughout the country banks, businesses, and farms failed, and the number of destitute families climbed into the millions. By 1933, 25 percent of the work force was unemployed, swamping the hopelessly inadequate private and state relief agencies. A complacent government, trapped in the delusion that prosperity was just around the corner, did little to relieve the distress. Rumblings from among the impoverished and the dispossessed grew more insistent as a revived political left began to act.

One of the Depression's first casualties was the art market. Collectors stopped buying and major patrons such as Gertrude Vanderbilt Whitney, Mrs. John D. Rockefeller, and Duncan Phillips reined in their spending. Dozens of art galleries went under and those that survived did so with great difficulty. A whole generation of aspiring painters and sculptors had no prospects, and even work by well-established figures lacked buyers. Growing frustration and despair led many artists to a new-found identification with other victims of the Depression—men deprived of employment or whole families living in privation. "The early 1930s were coldly sobering years," the painter Louis Guglielmi recalled later in the decade. "Faced with the terror of the realities of the day, [the artist] could no longer justify the shaky theory of individualism and the role of spectator." As he wrote, Guglielmi concluded that "The time has come when painters are returning to the life of the people once again and by so doing are absorbing the richness, the vitality, and the lusty healthiness inherent in the people."[5]

In these circumstances, an art of social content and wide accessibility gained favor. The extraordinary burst of social consciousness in the art community of the century's early years had already set the stage for the larger, more intensively pursued concept of a "people's art" in the 1930s. Urban and industrial themes, representations of worn or defiant workers, and depictions of social dislocation reflected artists' efforts to express their solidarity with the working class. Nor did artists confine themselves to

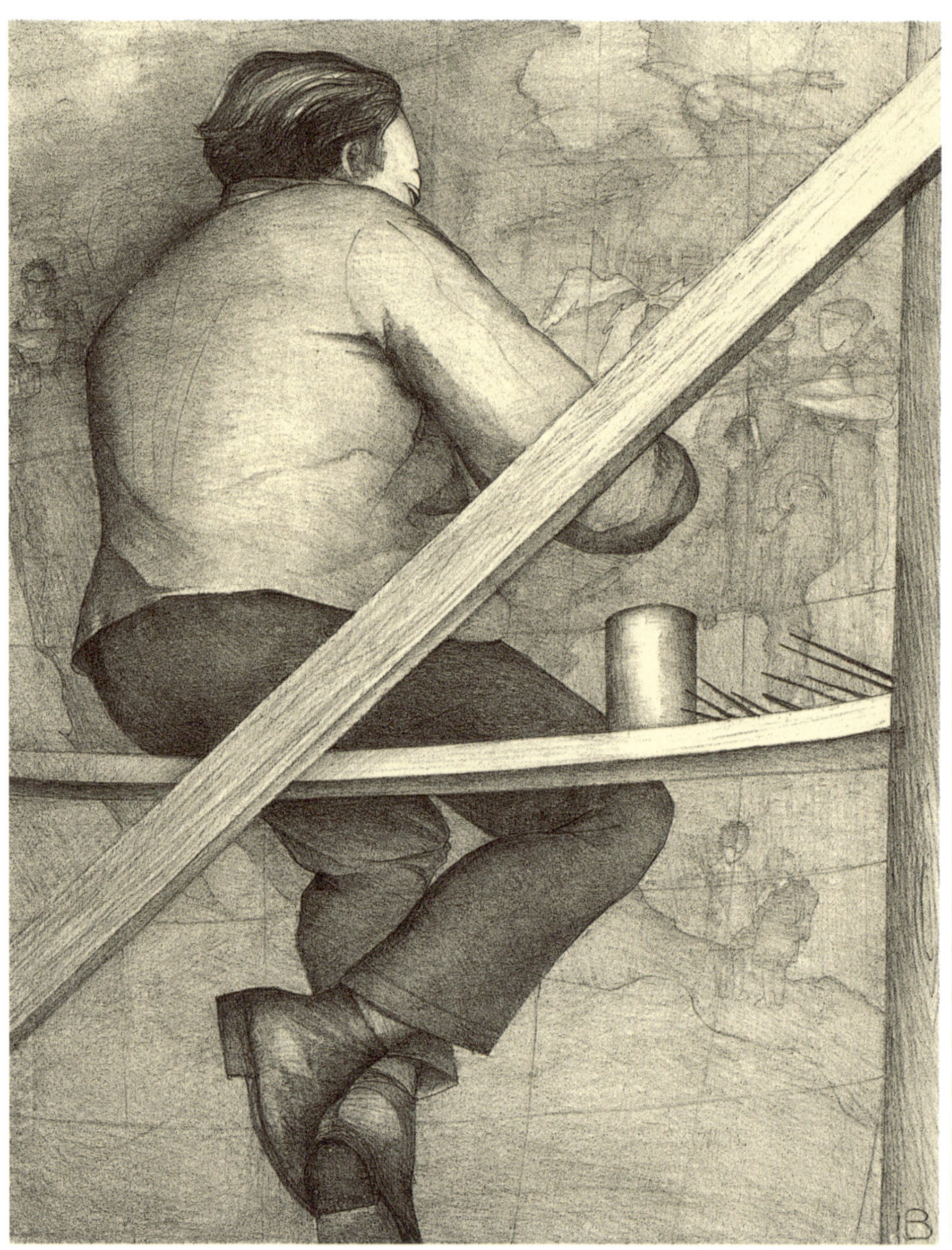

their studios. Political awareness and demands for solutions led to organized protest. The John Reed Club, founded in the fall of 1929 by artists and writers with ties to the *New Masses*, established an art school, sponsored Marxist-oriented lectures and discussions, and held exhibitions devoted to themes of social protest. Some of its members—for instance, Stuart Davis, Hugo Gellert, and William Gropper—had been contributors to *The Masses* and the *Liberator* ten and twenty years earlier. Some members of the John Reed Club organized several other organizations. The Artists Committee for Action led protests against the destruction of Diego Rivera's Rockefeller Center

Figure 15
LUCIENNE BLOCH. *Diego Rivera.*
Lithograph. Ca. 1933.
Courtesy Old Stage Studios,
Gualala, California 95445.

The influence of the Mexican muralists on American artists took tangible form in the work of Lucienne Bloch, who, with her husband Stephen Pope Dimitroff, assisted Diego Rivera in creating murals in Detroit and New York between 1931 and 1933, among them Rivera's controversial murals for Rockefeller Center.

mural, torn down because it included a portrait of Lenin, and called for the establishment of a municipal art gallery in New York. The Unemployed Artists' Group first agitated for public employment programs for artists and then transformed itself into a broader lobbying and pressure group, the Artists' Union. As one member recalled the Artists' Union: "You belonged simply because issues that were vital to your well being and your job were discussed there. . . . It was a mixture of tremendous seriousness, political awareness, great leadership, and very unexpected things that would happen. You went to a meeting. . . and suddenly you found that you were in a sit-in and that you were going to be there for two days."[6]

Soon after Franklin D. Roosevelt and his administration took office in 1933, the first of several federal art programs began to take shape. The largest, best known, and most productive was the Federal Art Project, under the Works Progress Administration or WPA, which operated from 1935 to 1943 as a relief agency. By the time it ended, thousands of painters, sculptors, and printmakers throughout the country had been on its payroll. Its goals and procedures were decidedly democratic—any professional artist

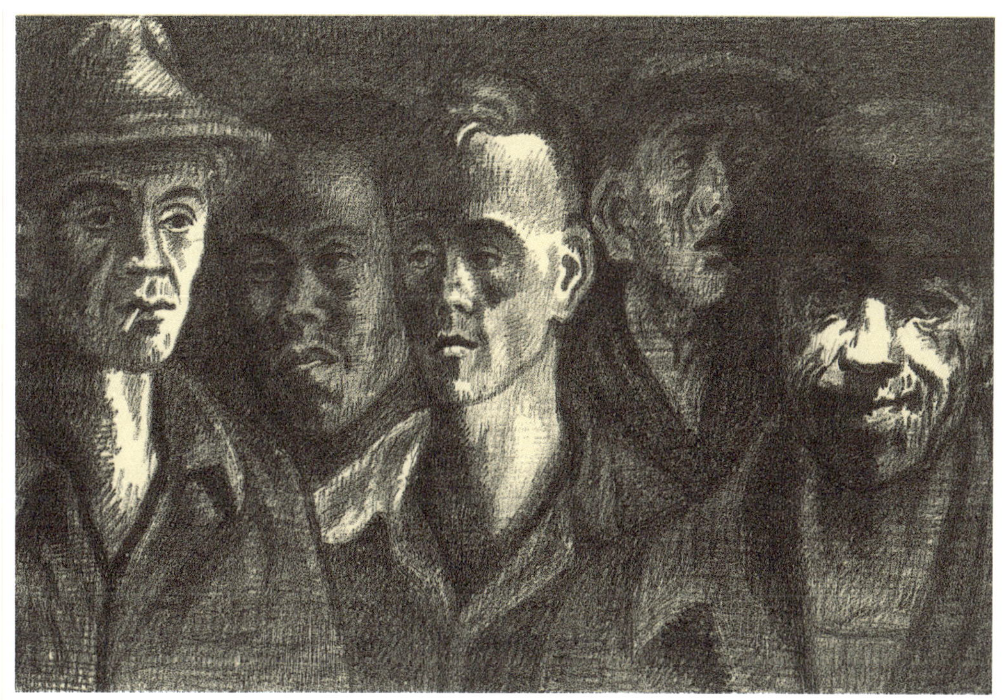

Figure 16
MOSES SOYER. *Defense Workers.*
Lithograph. 1942-43.
Copyright © Estate of Moses Soyer /
Licensed by VAGA, New York, N.Y.

Moses Soyer, twin brother of Raphael, enrolled in the WPA Federal Art Project as a painter in 1935. Best known for his work in this medium, he explored many genres from portraits to landscapes as a social realist. His lithograph *Defense Workers*, also called *War Workers*, sensitively depicts the faces of workers involved in the war effort.

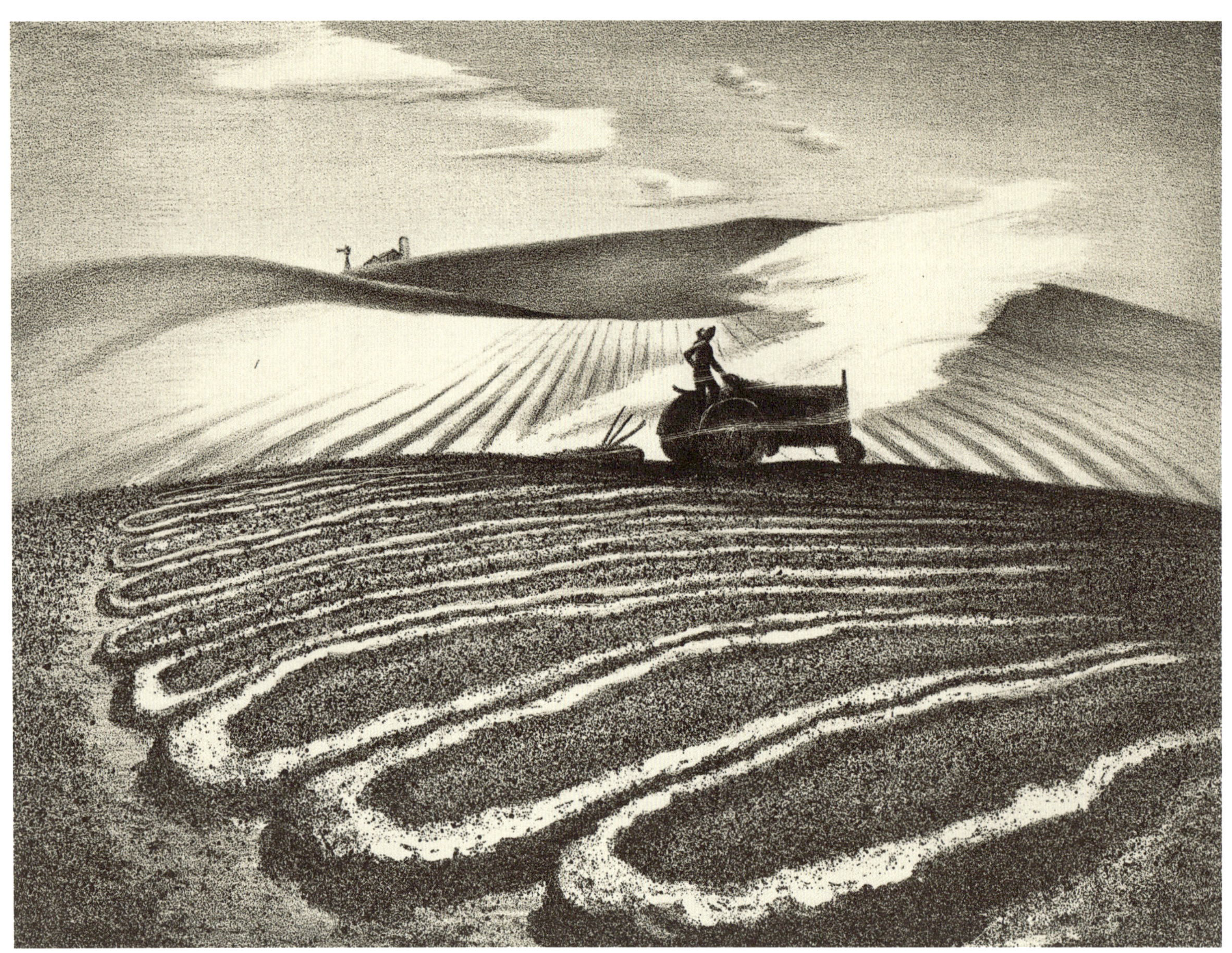

without means of support could get a modest but living wage in return for delivering a work of art every few weeks. The works produced were assigned to public places such as schools, hospitals, libraries, or housing projects.

The conditions of the time found expression through the federal art programs, whose nature and purposes fostered the depictions of ordinary life that poured out of the studios in a genuine response to the world around the artists. In a typical reminiscence of the 1930s, Anton Refregier, whose *San Francisco '34 Waterfront Strike* (pl. 12) celebrates one of the most successful labor actions of the decade, recalls: "The years I

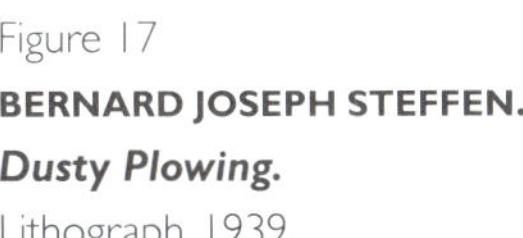

Figure 17
BERNARD JOSEPH STEFFEN.
Dusty Plowing.
Lithograph. 1939.

A native of Kansas, Bernard Steffen brought a rural sensibility to New York, where he studied under Thomas Hart Benton at the Art Students League. Benton's influence is evident in *Dusty Plowing*, which Steffen created for the New York City WPA Federal Art Project. Steffen, however, focused on landscape and eschewed the romance and narrative that marked the Regionalists.

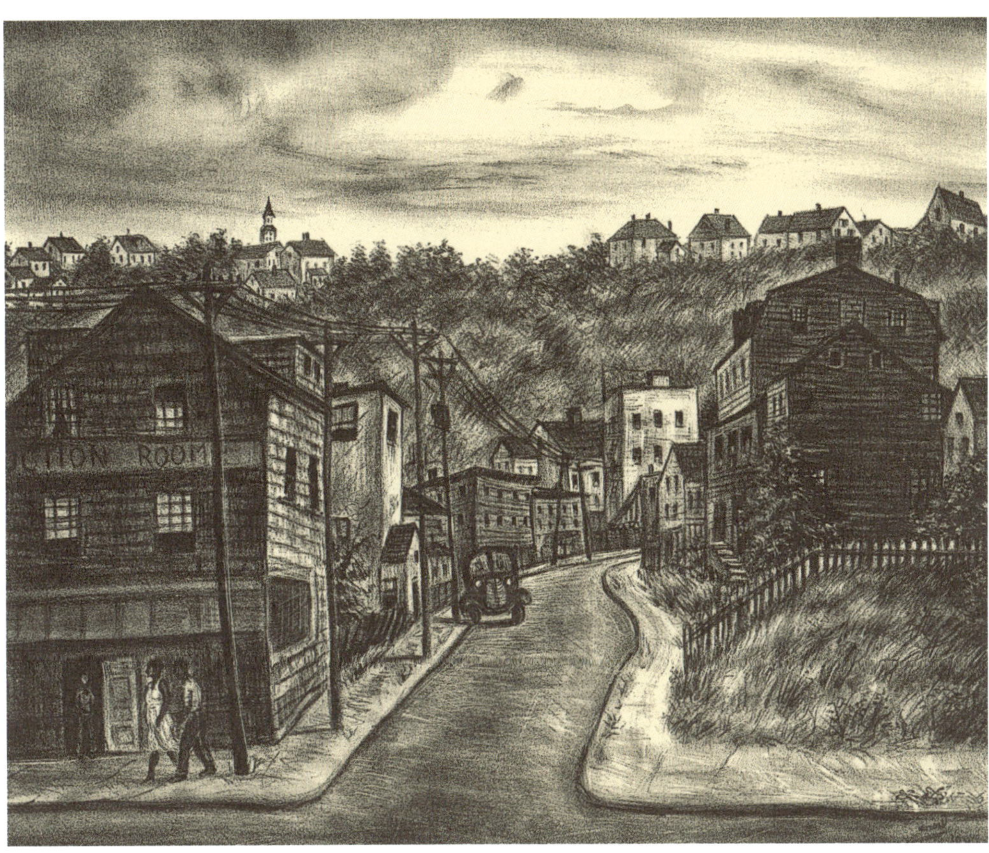

Figure 18
SAUL KOVNER. *Small Town Harlem.*
Lithograph. 1940.

Russian-born Saul Kovner, who typically dropped his surname when signing prints, captured the surprisingly rural, small-town atmosphere of a Harlem neighborhood in this print produced for the New York City WPA Federal Art Project.

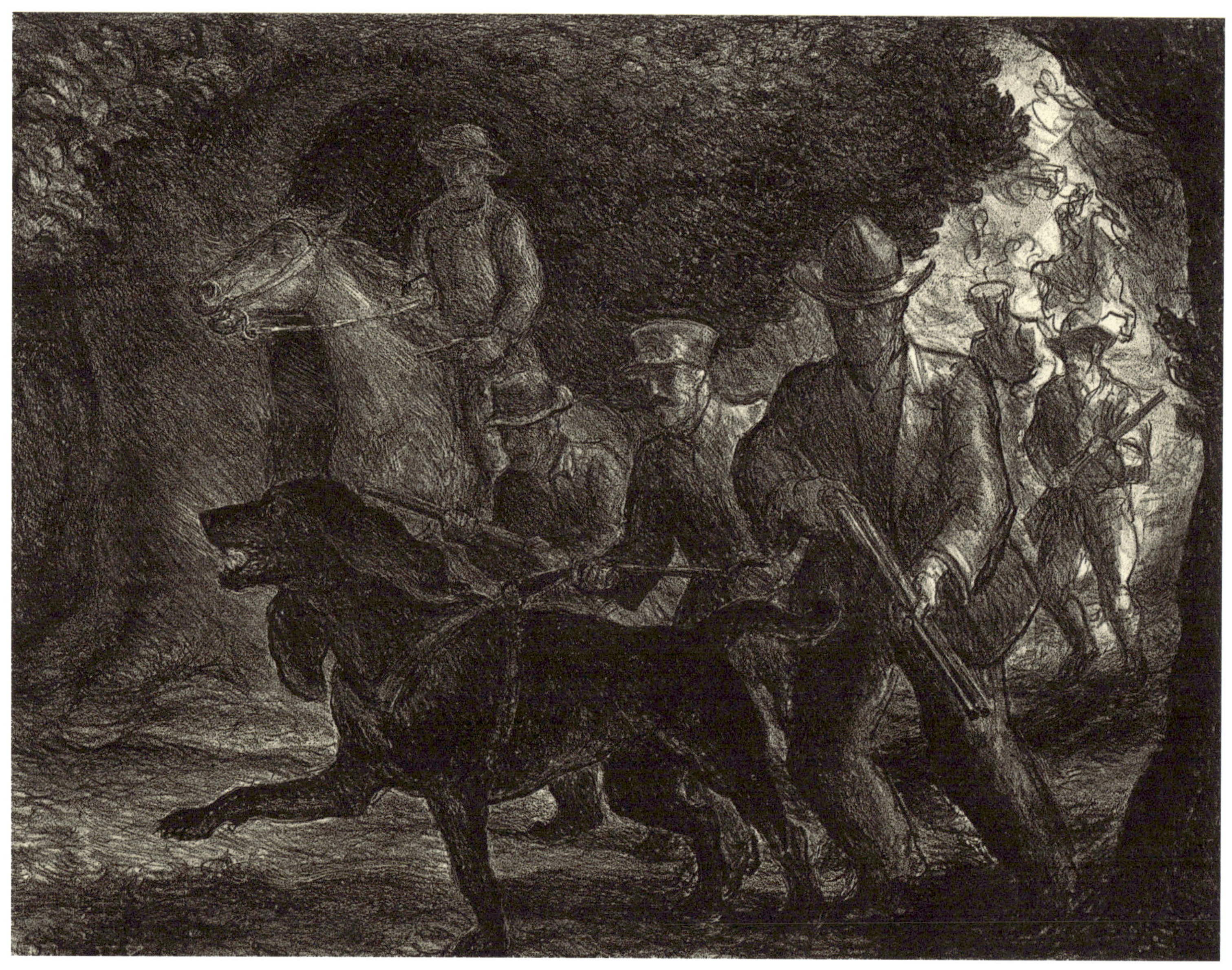

worked on the WPA Art Project were the most meaningful and the happiest of my professional life. I felt a sense of purpose, a closeness to the people with whom we shared our economic plight, a feeling of being needed by them."[7]

In Mexico, in a striking parallel manifestation of this same populist impulse, a vibrant public art reflecting the life and history of the Mexican people sprang up in the 1920s as a cultural legacy of the Mexican Revolution. Its leading figures—Diego Rivera (pl.17), José Clemente Orozco (fig. 34), and David Siqueiros—were well known in the United States, where they painted controversial murals in the 1930s. Their assertive radicalism, formal experimentation, and insistence

Figure 19
JOHN STEUART CURRY. *Manhunt.*
Lithograph. 1934.
Reproduction courtesy of
Mrs. John Steuart Curry.

The darker side of the Regionalist vision of America is evident in John Steuart Curry's many powerful and dramatic depictions of the African American experience. *Manhunt*, a variation on a 1931 painting of the same title, shows a lynch mob in action in Kansas.

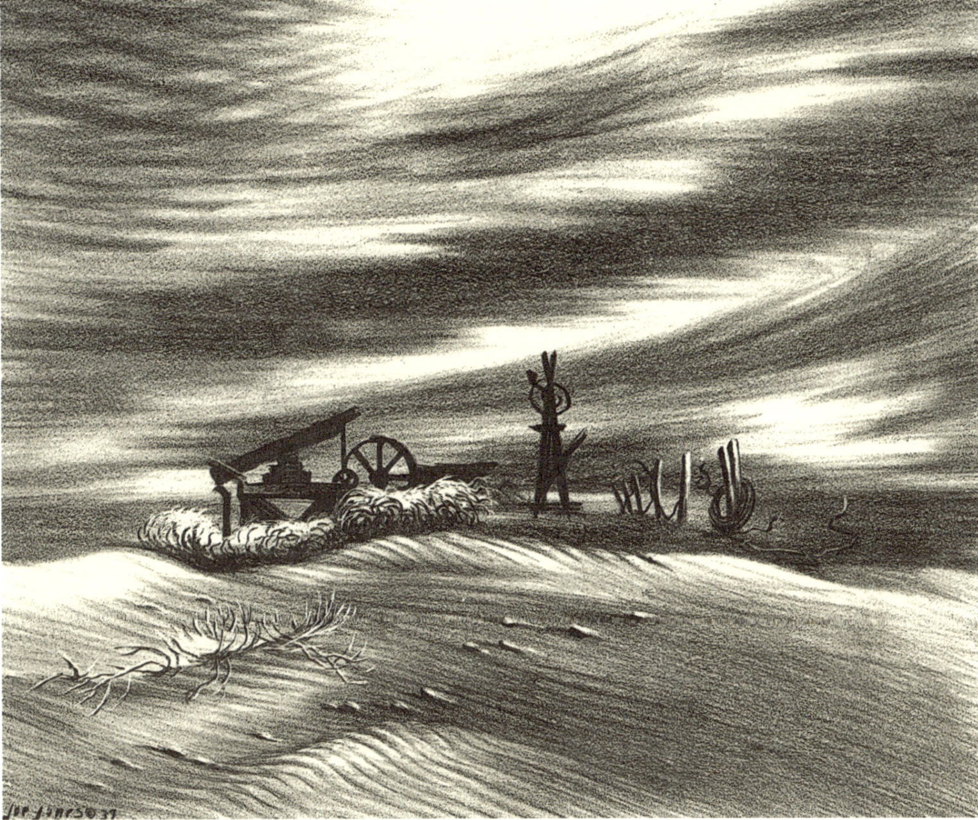

Figure 20
JOE JONES. *Wastelands.*
Lithograph. 1937.
Reproduction courtesy of
Grace Adams Jones.

In 1937 Joe Jones received a Guggenheim fellowship to create a pictorial record of conditions in the dust bowl, of which *Wastelands* is an example.

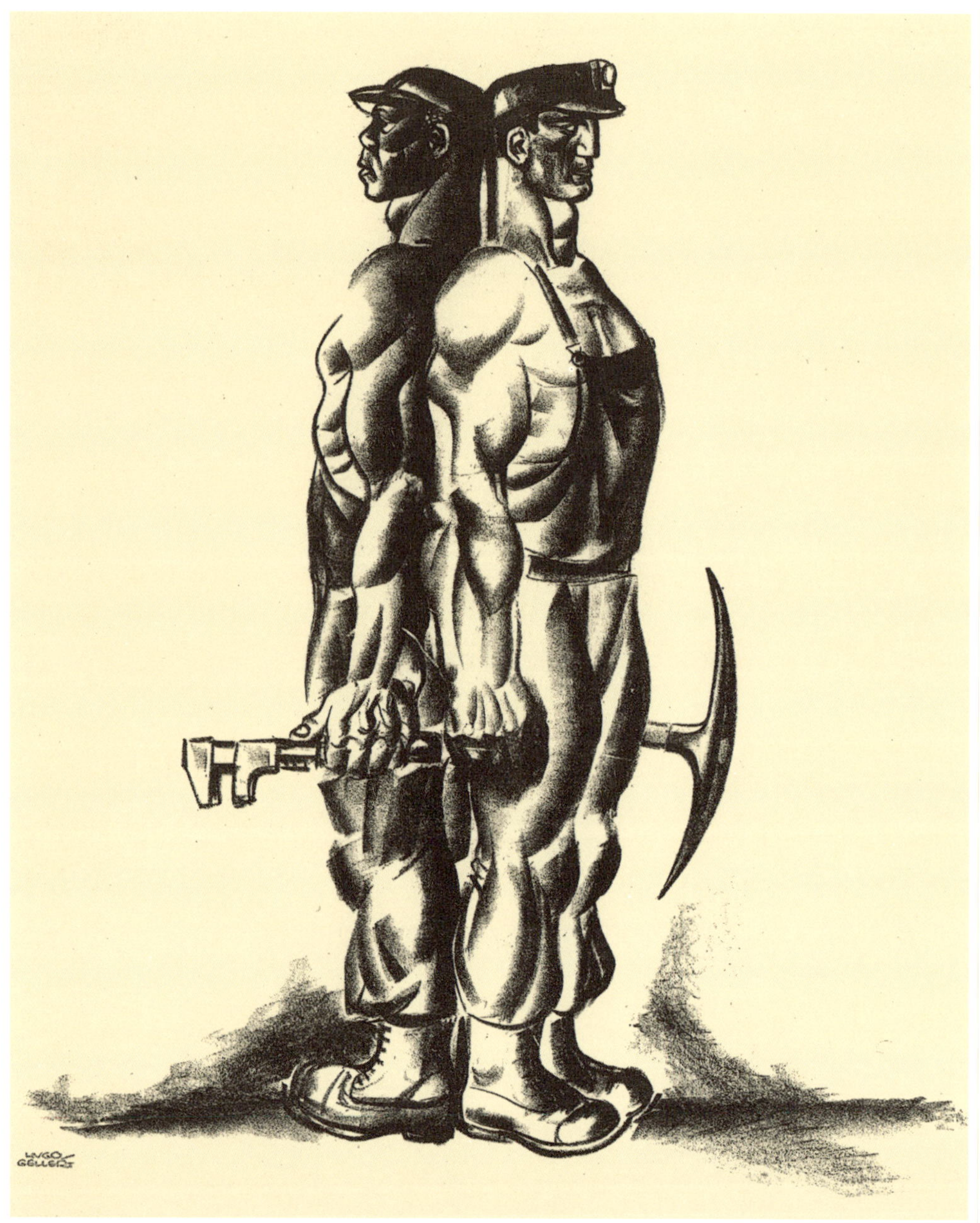

Figure 21

HUGO GELLERT. *The Working Day*, no. 37.
Lithograph. Ca. 1933.
Reproduction courtesy of
the Estate of Hugo Gellert.

Hugo Gellert considered his politics insepa-
rable from his art, arguing that "Being an
artist and being a communist are one and
the same. One is as important as the
other." *The Working Day*, which features a
white miner and a black industrial worker,
is part of the portfolio *Karl Marx in Pictures*
that Gellert published in France in 1933
with text from *Das Kapital*, which reads in
part, "Labor with a white skin cannot
emancipate itself where labor with a black
skin is branded."

Figure 22

MICHAEL LENSON. *Full Production and
Full Employment under Our Democratic
System of Private Enterprise.*
Crayon and ink. Ca. 1944.
Reproduction courtesy of Barry Lenson
and David Lenson.

Unusual among the images in the Goldstein
Collection in extolling without reservation
the benefits of capitalism, Michael Lenson's
drawing exhibits elements of cartooning
and surrealistic distortion. Lenson's title is a
quotation from Franklin Delano Roosevelt's
campaign speech at a union dinner in
Washington, D.C., on September 23, 1944.

on accessible imagery struck a responsive chord in American artists seeking ways to express solidarity with the life of their own people. A younger, but equally dedicated colleague, Pablo O'Higgins (fig. 30), was an expatriate American (Paul Higgins), who trained under Rivera, lived most of his life in Mexico, and painted murals in union halls in Seattle and Honolulu.

For artists with a strong sense of moral indignation there were plenty of themes to address. Lynchings, strikes, poverty, bread-lines, tenement life, and rural hardships were common subjects, as was the Spanish Civil War. We see these themes, for example, in John Steuart Curry's *Manhunt* (fig. 19), in Joe Jones's *Wasteland* (fig. 20), and in Georges Schreiber's *From Arkansas* (pl. 19). The dignity of work and of workers is reflected in Harry Sternberg's *Builders* (fig. 2) and *Coal Miners* and in Joseph Hirsch's forceful *Lunch Hour* (pl. 20). Hugo Gellert's lithograph of a miner back-to-back with an industrial worker, *The Working Day,* is an idealized picture that could have been pro-duced only in the 1930s. Michael Lenson's *Full Production and Full Employment under Our Democratic System of Private Enterprise* seems an ideological anomaly among so many

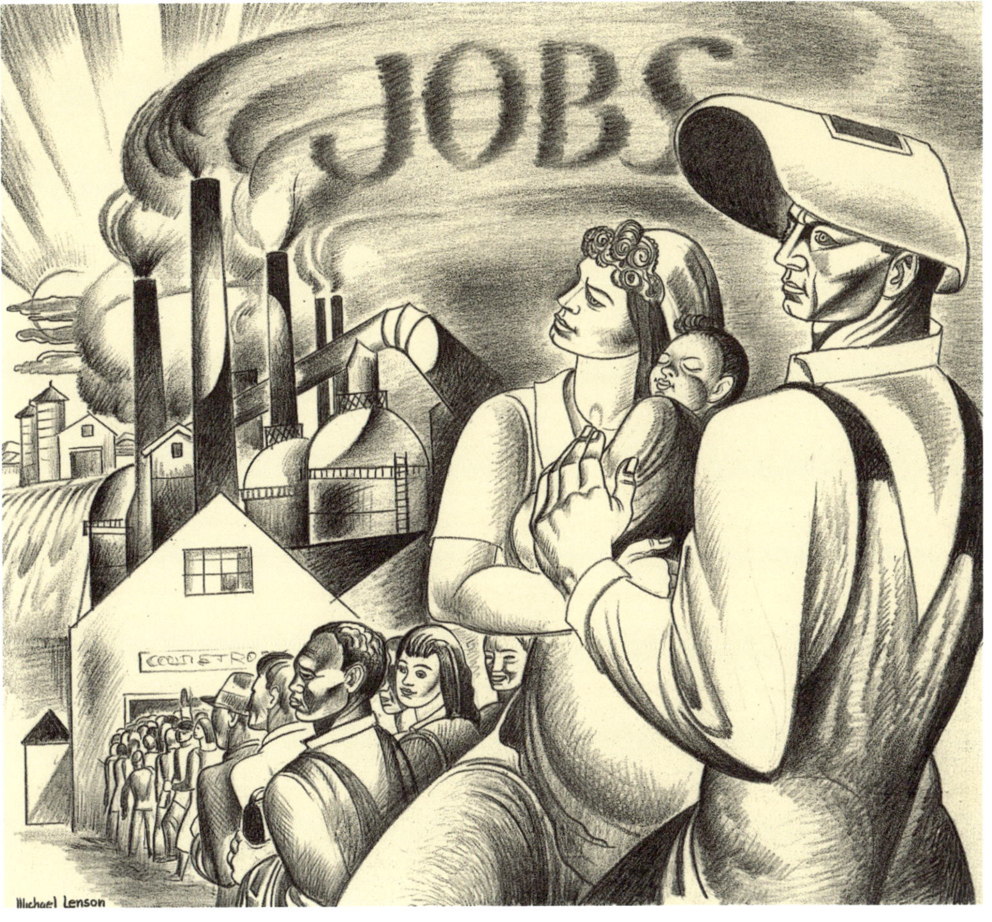

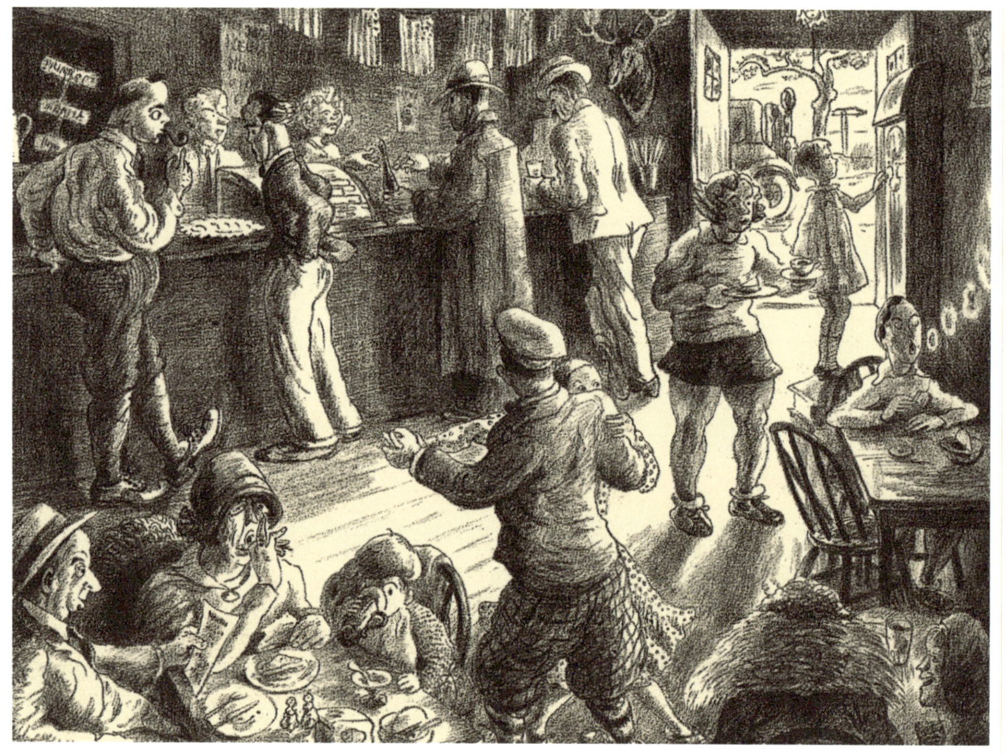

critical depictions of harsh economic conditions.

The transition from the twenties to the thirties is exemplified in two lithographs by Mabel Dwight, one of the best printmakers of the time. Her image *The Clinch, Movie Theatre* (pl. 7) of 1928 is a lighthearted look at romance. In contrast, three years later in her lithograph *In the Crowd* (pl. 8) Dwight depicted a group of somber, worried men and women. We find a continuation of the earlier satirical vein in Peggy Bacon's *Rural Retreat* and Elizabeth Olds's *White Collar Boys*.

The Depression drew to a close with the

Figure 23
PEGGY BACON. *Rural Retreat.*
Lithograph. 1930.
Reproduction courtesy of
the Estate of Peggy Bacon.

The Log Cabin, a roadhouse in Cross River, Westchester County, New York, where Peggy Bacon and her husband Alexander Brook made their summer home from 1927 until 1937, provided the setting for *Rural Retreat*.

Figure 24
ELIZABETH OLDS. *White Collar Boys.*
Lithograph. 1936.
Reproduction courtesy of
the Estate of Elizabeth Olds.

Elizabeth Olds's sense of humor and careful study of satirical works by Honoré Daumier, William Glackens, and William Gropper are evident in this lithograph. She portrays the scurrying businessmen, or "white collar boys" of the title, as undifferentiated types rather than as distinct individuals.

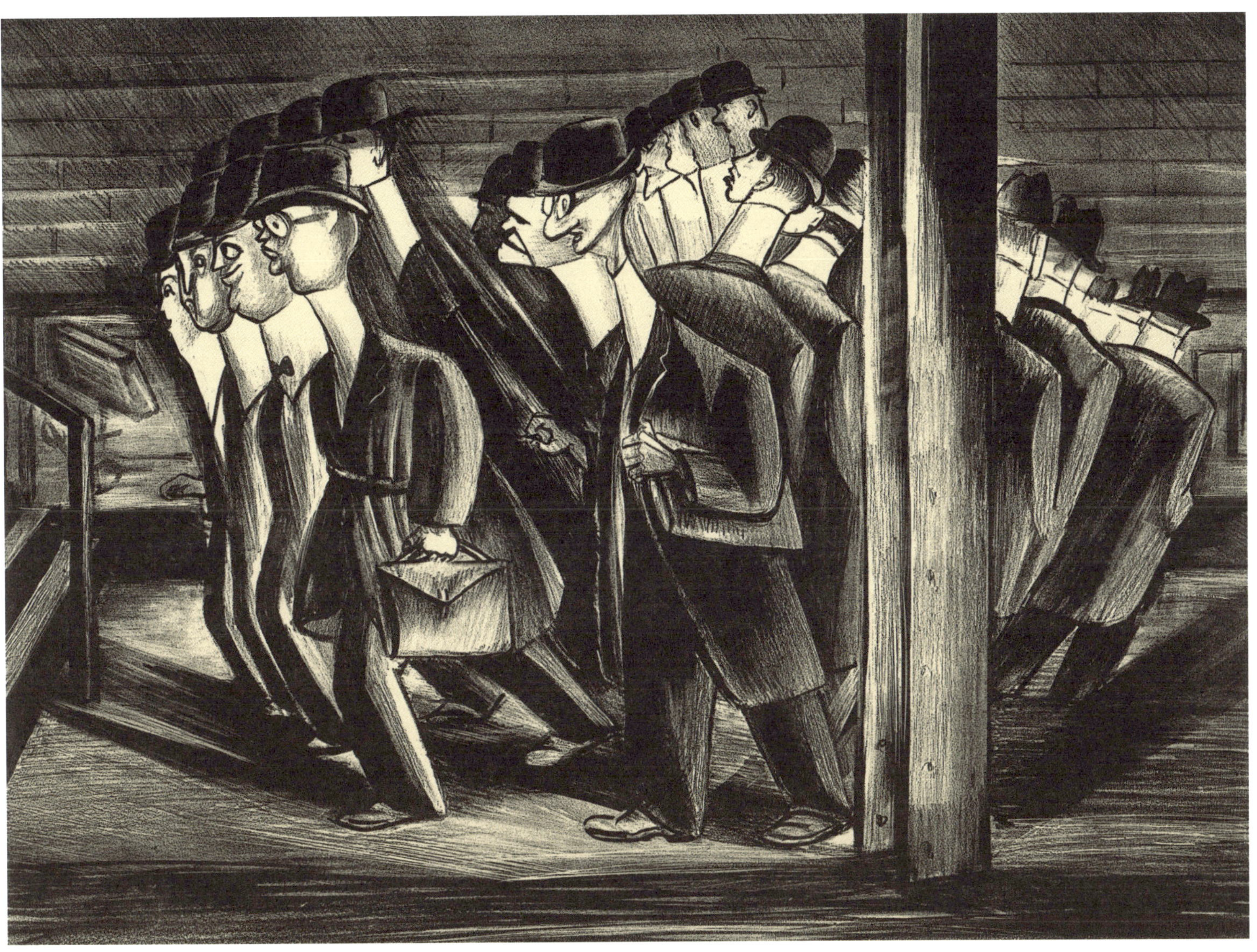

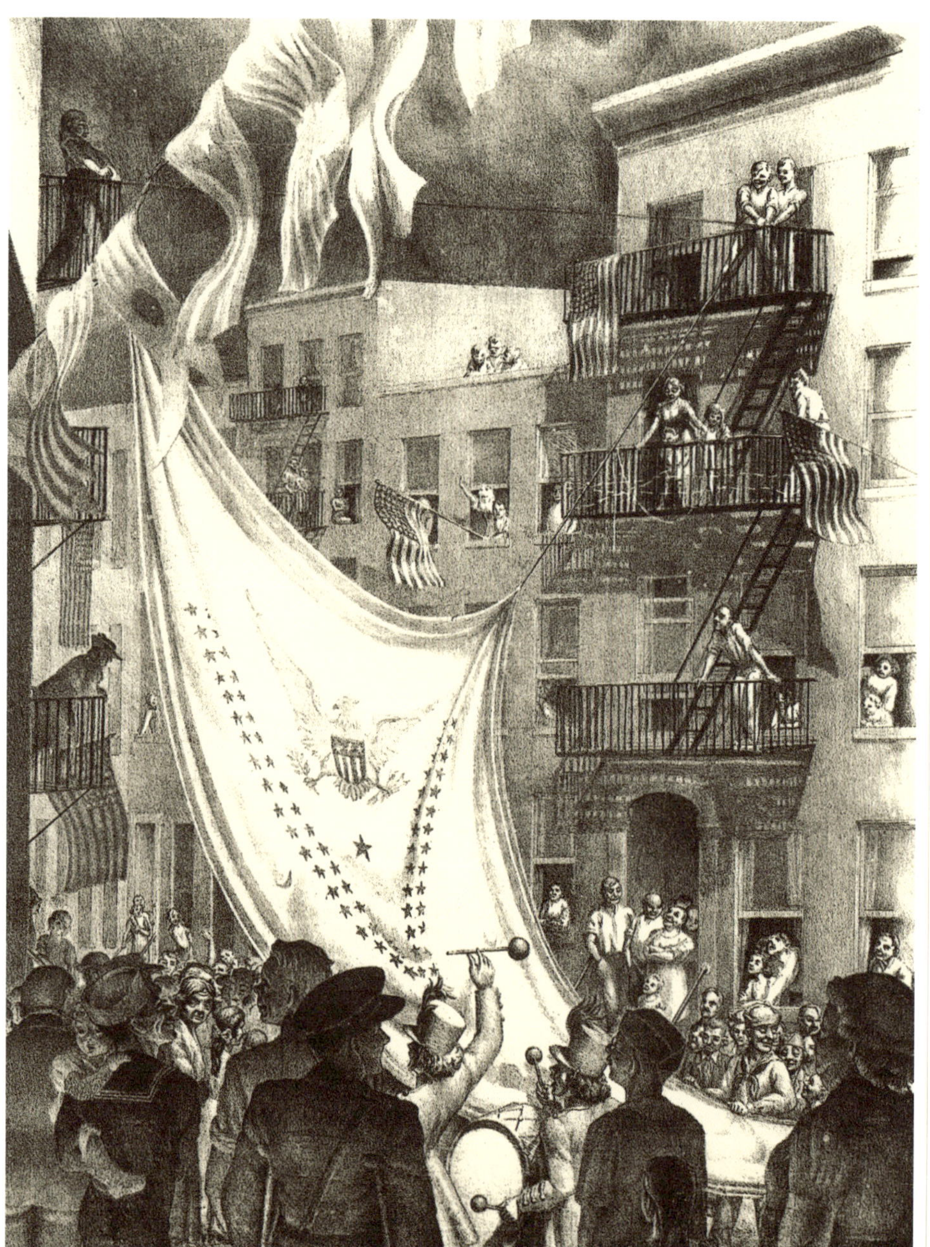

Figure 25

KYRA MARKHAM.
Flag Raising in Leroy St.
Lithograph. 1942.

During World War II, Kyra Markham and many other artists in the United States contributed to the war effort by creating images that stirred patriotic sentiments and feelings of contentment toward life in America. Markham viewed lithography as an extension of drawing and wielded the lithographic crayon with the same sensitivity and skill that many artists achieve only with the pencil.

Figure 26

LOUIS LOZOWICK. *Guts of Manhattan.*
Lithograph. 1939.
Reproduction courtesy of Adele Lozowick.

During the Depression, Louis Lozowick took advantage of the unprecedented opportunity offered by the WPA Federal Art Project, joining the Graphic Arts Division between 1938 and 1940. Realism and abstraction blend brilliantly in *Guts of Manhattan*, in which Lozowick sketched the underground work he could see through the scaffolding during the construction of subway lines along Sixth and Eighth Avenues.

rise of wartime industrial production in 1940. After the United States entered World War II, the defense effort became a prominent subject for artists. Kyra Markham's *Flag Raising in Leroy St.* reveals its setting to be a neighborhood during wartime. Charles White's *The Return of the Soldier* (pl. 18) revives the bitter commentary on racial injustice.

Since an art of social protest finds in realism its most effective and most accessible manner of presentation, most of the memorable work of social concern takes that form. One exception among the works shown here is Louis Lozowick's complex lithograph *Guts of Manhattan*, picturing a welder with cables, which demonstrates how industrial subject matter lends itself to a more abstract treatment. In the same manner, the shaky skyscrapers in James N. Rosenberg's *Oct 29 Dies Irae* (Day of Wrath, pl. 6) provide a surreal take on the Wall Street stock market crash.

With renewed prosperity and the revival of the art market after World War II, a general reaction against 1930s attitudes and values swept through the art community. Conditions that had nourished protest, satire, and compassion in the arts no longer

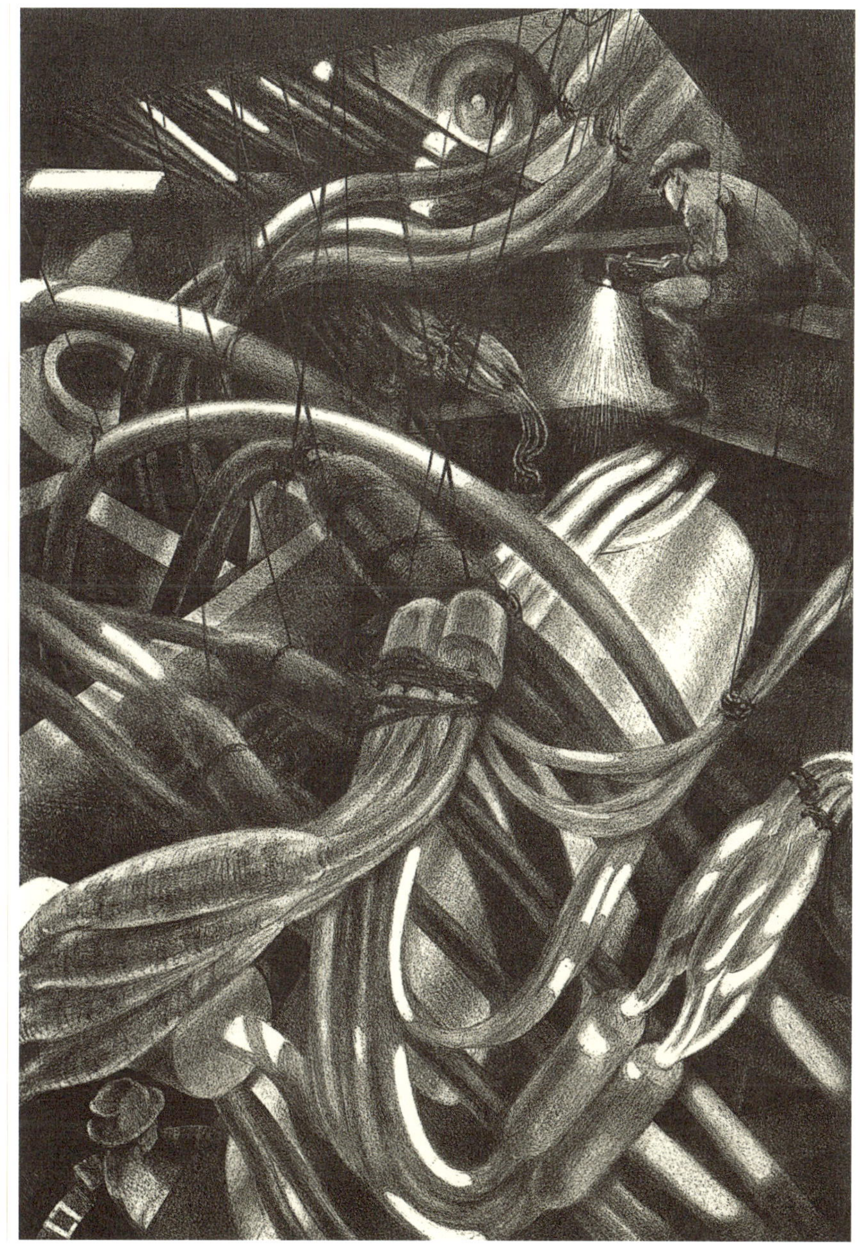

pertained in the postwar world, and artists who remained loyal to a socially oriented esthetic fell from critical favor as abstract expressionism triumphed over social realism. The old political battles and the old responses meant little to a rising generation with a different outlook and a different set of problems.

If economic and social conditions changed after the war, so did the political climate. The onset of the cold war, congressional witch-hunts, FBI investigations, state and federal loyalty programs, and the blacklisting of radicals in the entertainment and cultural fields effectively isolated the old left and inhibited the expression of unpopular critical views. Suspect artists were interrogated and in some instances their works were removed from exhibitions. With some exceptions the older forms of a people's art lost their base of support.

"The chilling effect of the cold war on artists," Ben Goldstein wrote to Rockwell Kent in 1969, "plus normal attrition have made collecting very difficult." Nevertheless, the collector persisted in searching out prints and drawings from the earlier period, and we can be grateful for his persistence. A significant aspect of our history and our art comes to life for us through his efforts.

NOTES

1. Ben Goldstein to Rockwell Kent, September 19, 1969, Rockwell Kent Papers, Archives of American Art, Smithsonian Institution, Washington, D.C.

2. From notes of John Sloan's observations and reminiscences, compiled by Helen Farr Sloan and quoted in Rebecca Zurier, *Art for the Masses* (Philadelphia: Temple University Press, 1988), 127.

3. Quoted in Zurier, *Art for the Masses*, 154.

4. Quoted, ibid., 138.

5. Louis Guglielmi, "After the Locusts," in Francis V. O'Connor, ed., *Art for the Millions: Essays from the 1930s by Artists and Administrators of the WPA Federal Art Project* (Greenwich, Conn.: New York Graphic Society, 1973), 113.

6. Abram Lerner, tape recorded interview, December 1975, p. 27, Archives of American Art, Smithsonian Institution.

7. Quoted in Patricia Hills, *Social Concern and Urban Realism: American Painting in the 1930s* (Boston: Boston University Art Gallery, 1983), 11.

Portfolio

ROBERT GWATHMEY. *Non Fiction.*
Screenprint. 1945.
Copyright © Estate of Robert Gwathmey /
Licensed by VAGA, New York, N.Y.

Born in Richmond, Virginia, Robert Gwathmey drew
upon his experience as a child in the South in his
artistic portrayals of white and black sharecroppers.
In 1944 he received a grant that permitted him to
work with sharecroppers on a tobacco farm, experi-
encing firsthand the realities of their daily lives.

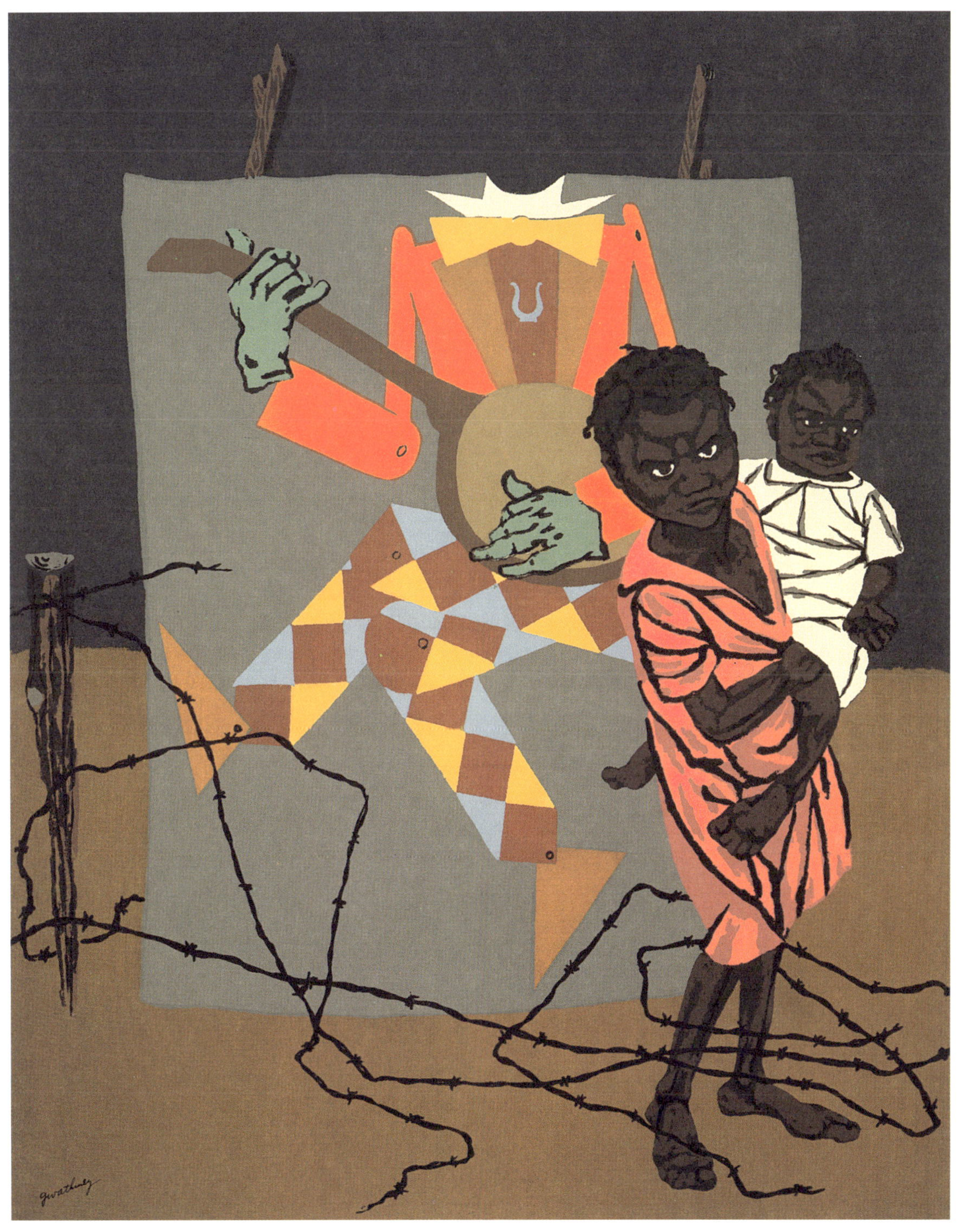

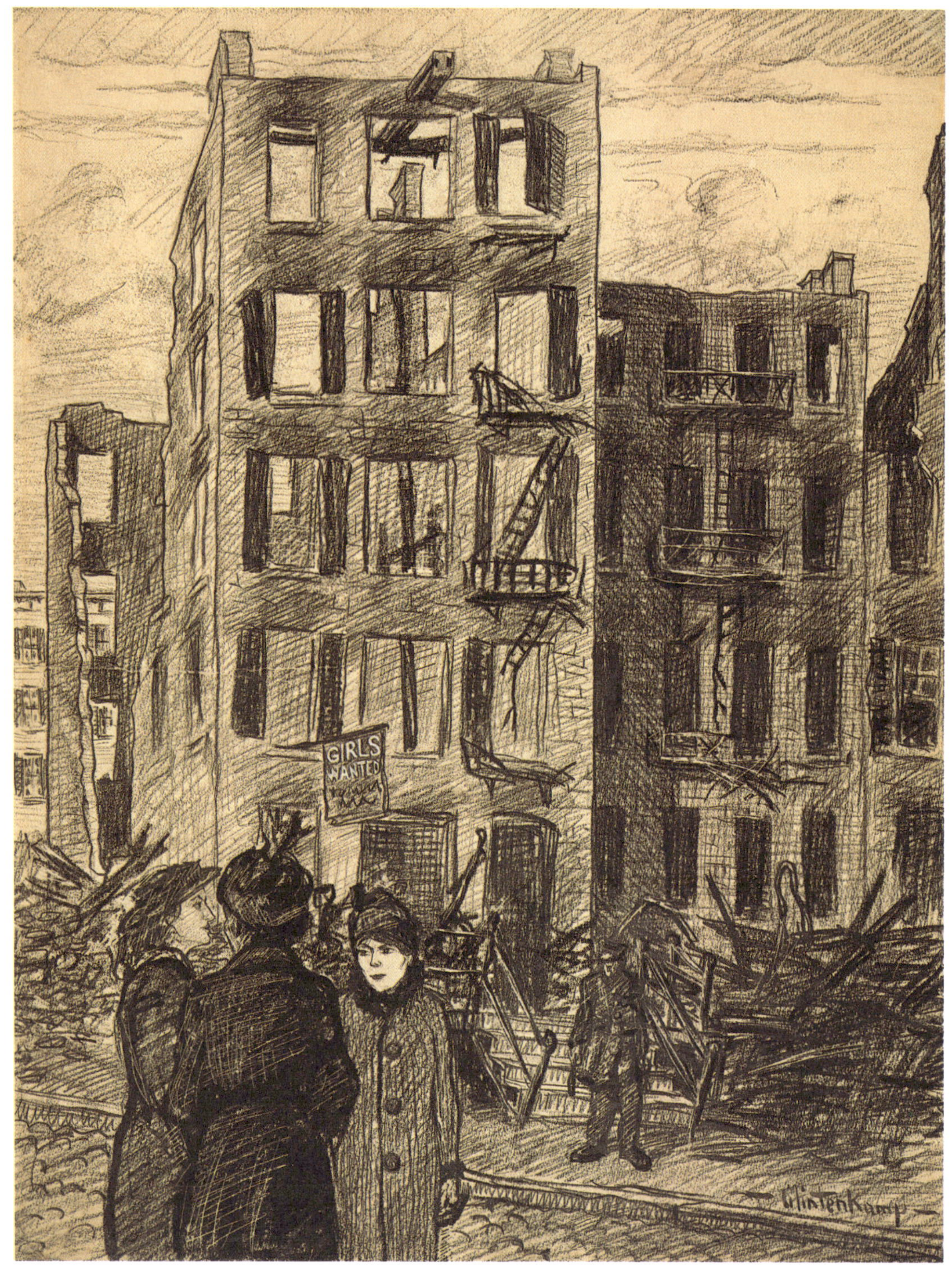
GIRLS
WANTED

HENRY GLINTENKAMP. *Girls Wanted.*
Crayon. 1916.

Girls Wanted comments on the tragic Triangle Shirtwaist Company Fire of 1911, which came to the
public's attention again in 1916 as investigators issued
their report. Henry Glintenkamp began contributing
drawings to the influential leftist magazine *The Masses*
in 1913 and remained a regular contributor through
1916, when *Girls Wanted* was published.

PLATE 3
ROBERT MINOR.
Morgan, Mellon, and Rockefeller.
Crayon and ink. Ca. 1922.

"Fighting Bob" Minor's politics are often evident in
his cartoons. A socialist with anarchist leanings
during the 1910s, Minor became a member of the
Communist Party in the 1920s, eventually giving up
cartooning for politics in 1926. In this small, savage
sketch, Minor caricatured the capitalist magnates
J. P. Morgan (left), Andrew Mellon (center), and John
D. Rockefeller (right) as avaricious men.

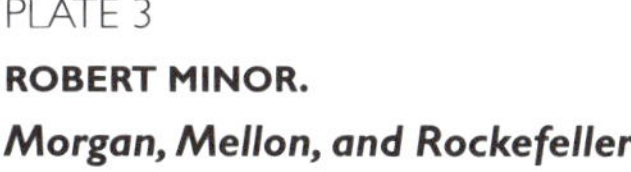

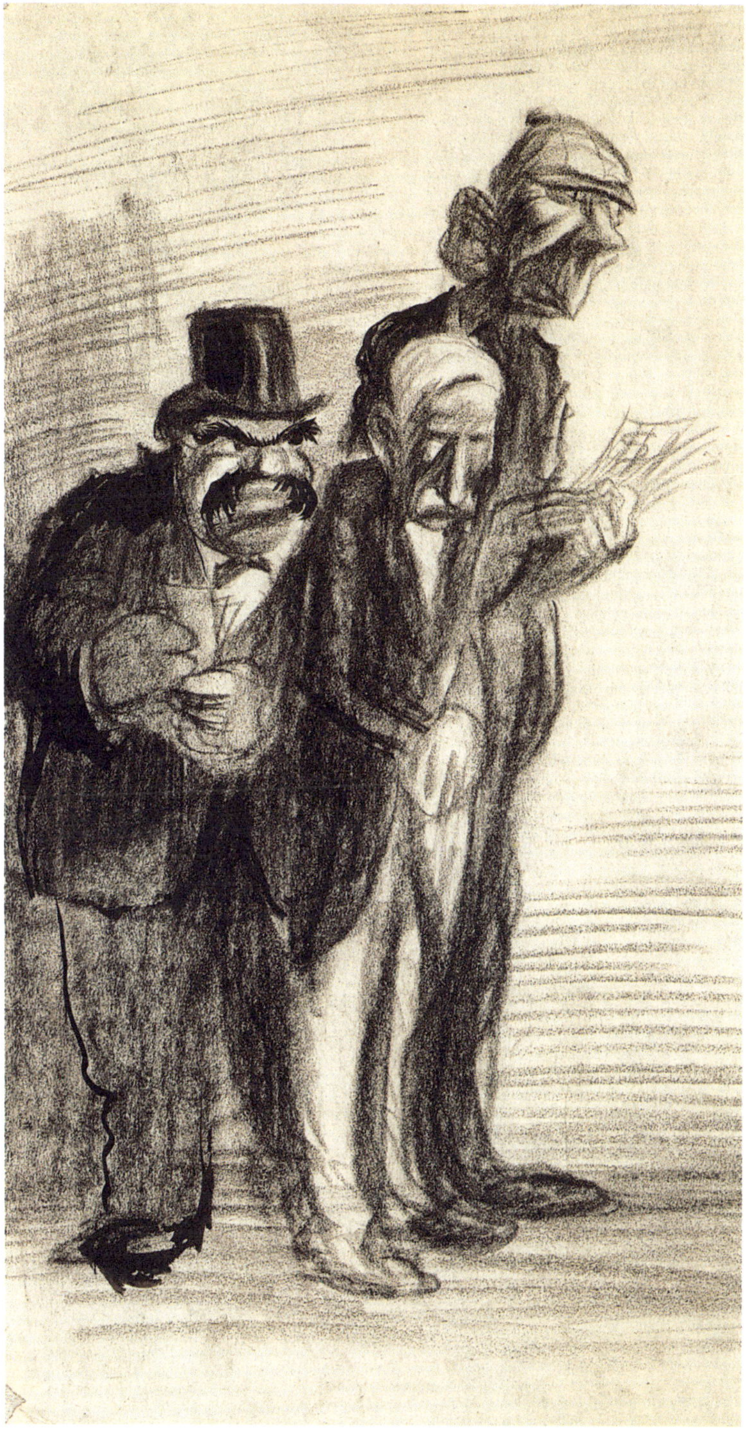

ELIZABETH OLDS. *Miner Joe.*
Screenprint. 1940.
Reproduction courtesy of
the Estate of Elizabeth Olds.

In the winter of 1938-39, Elizabeth Olds joined
Anthony Velonis and other WPA printmakers in
introducing the use of the commercial screenprint
process as a fine art medium. *Miner Joe* exemplifies
her mastery of the newly developed art form.

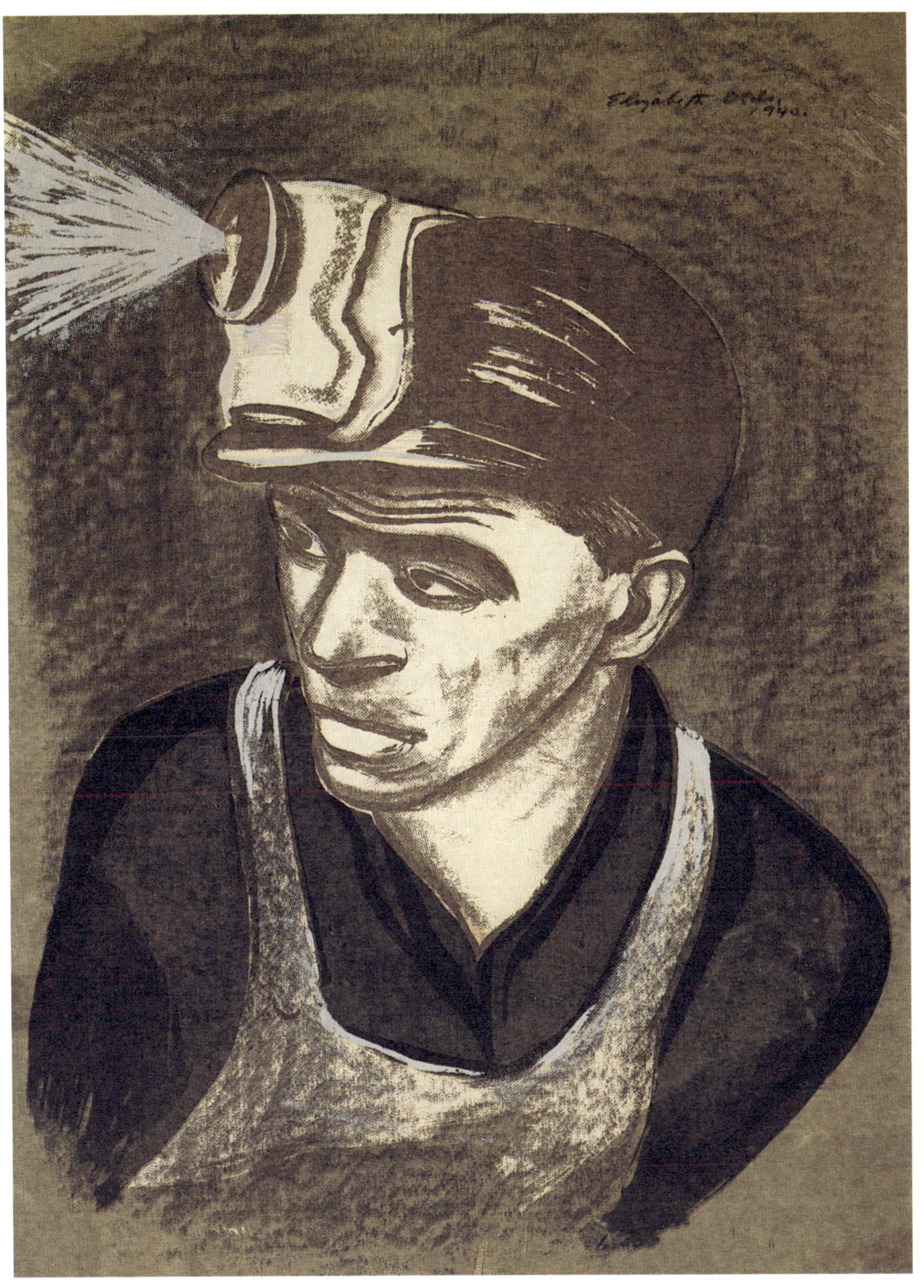

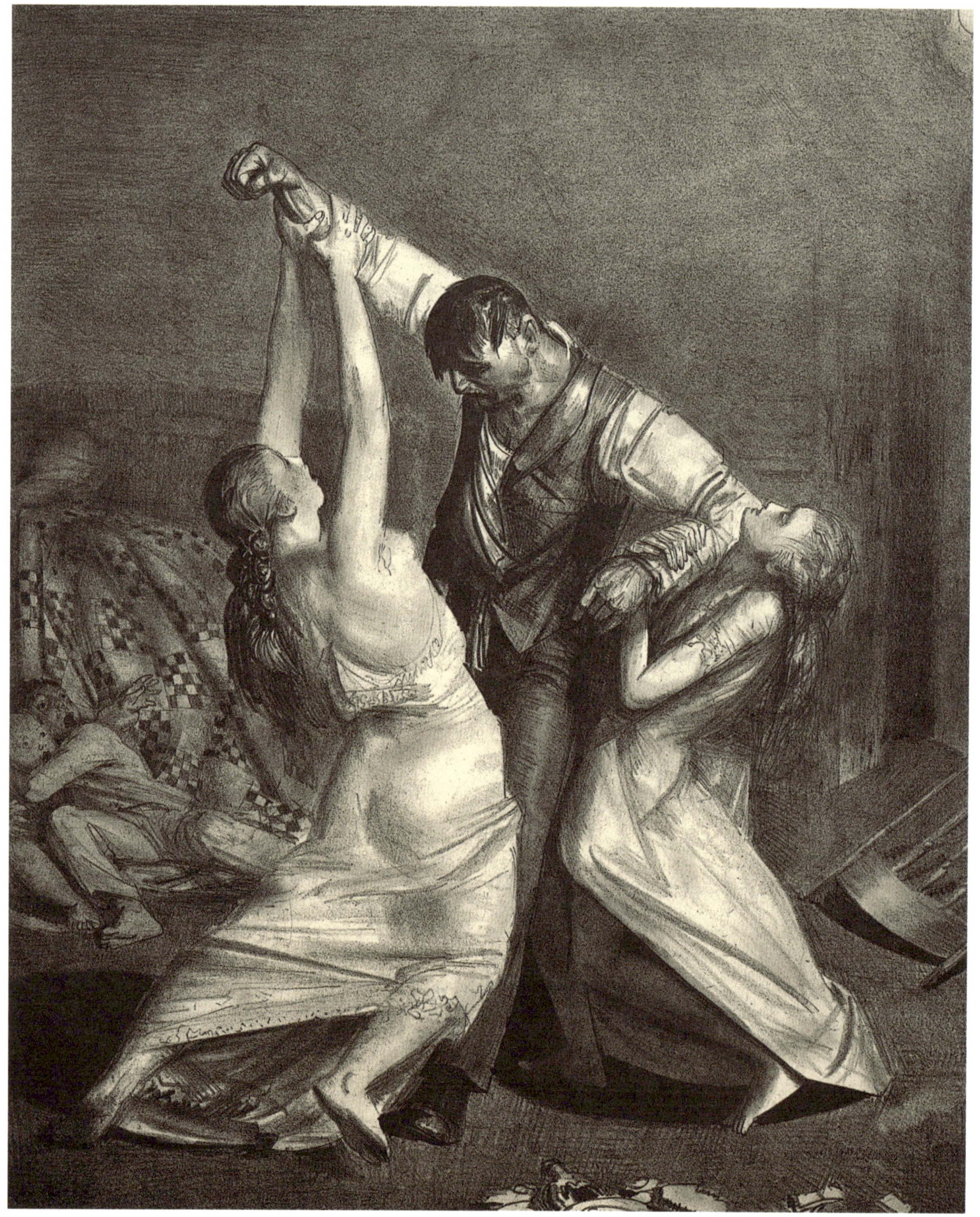

GEORGE BELLOWS. *The Drunk.*
Lithograph. Second state. Ca. 1924.
Reproduction courtesy of Mrs. Earl M. Booth.

George Bellows created this tense, violent image of
a wife struggling desperately to subdue her drunken
husband to illustrate an article entitled "Why We
Prohibit," which appeared in *Good Housekeeping* in
1924, in the midst of the Prohibition Era. *The Drunk*
epitomizes the triangular composition that charac-
terized Bellows's work from 1917 on, when he
adopted the principle of dynamic symmetry, a series
of geometric formulas used in the organization of a
picture. Like *In the Subway* (fig. 10), this lithograph was
printed by Bolton Brown in the printshop he had
established in Woodstock, New York, in 1919.

JAMES N. ROSENBERG. *Oct 29 Dies Irae.*
Lithograph. 1929.
Reproduction courtesy of
the Estate of James N. Rosenberg,
permission granted by Anne Geismar.

In *Dies Irae* (Day of Wrath), James Rosenberg
created an expressionist nightmare of teetering
skyscrapers, suicidal stockbrokers, storm clouds, and
maddened crowds to convey the sense of panic that
overwhelmed Wall Street and the nation in the last
days of October 1929. A bankruptcy lawyer in
Manhattan who also studied lithography under
master printmaker George Miller, Rosenberg
recalled: "In the afternoon of October 28 [*sic*], 1929,
the terrible day when nine million shares were
slaughtered on the New York Stock Exchange,
I rushed to Miller's place and made my lithograph
Dies Irae."

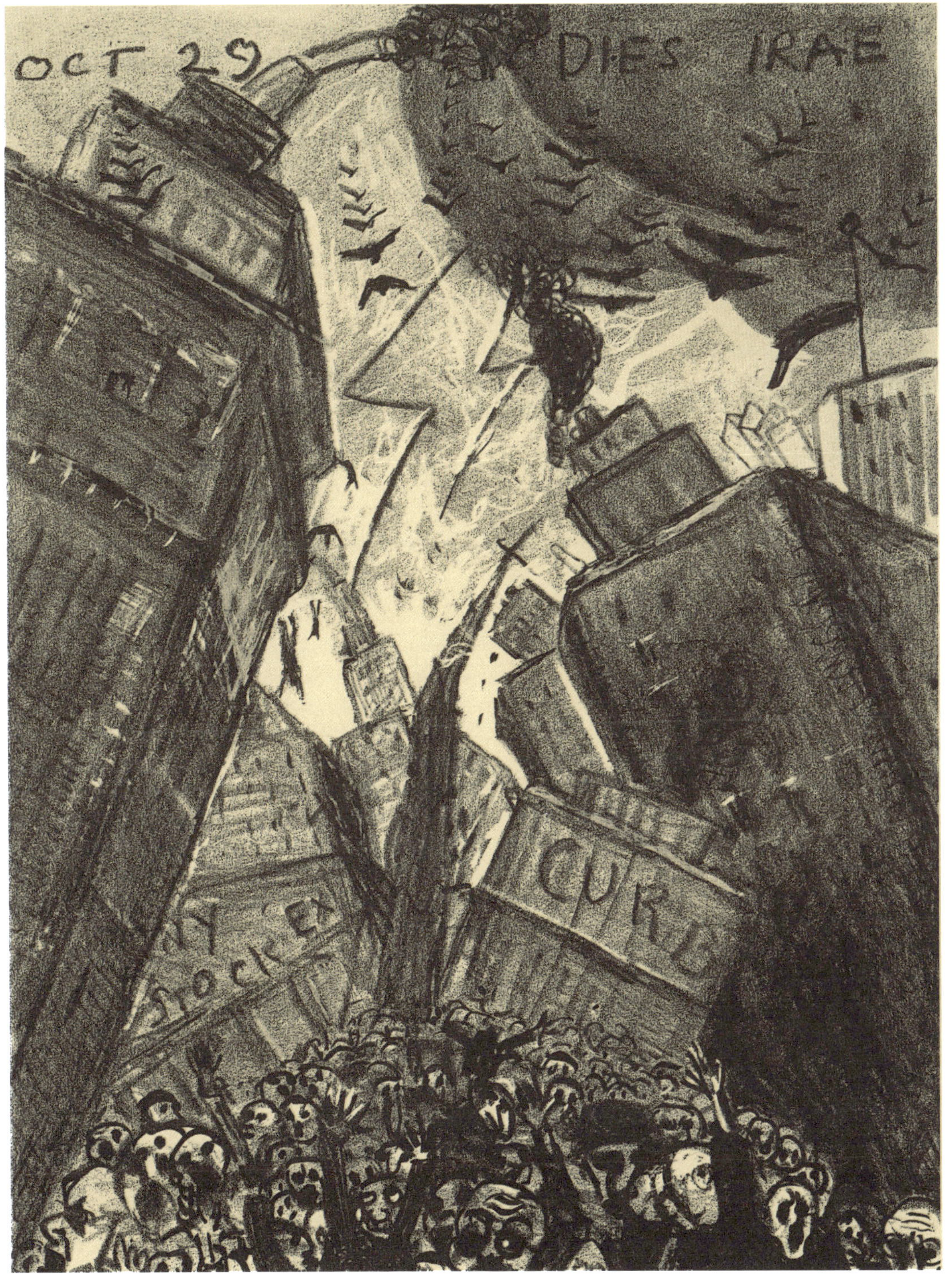

OCT 29   DIES IRAE
CURB
N.Y.
STOCK EX

MABEL DWIGHT. *The Clinch, Movie Theatre.*
Lithograph. Second state. 1928.

Hollywood came of age during the 1920s, and Mabel Dwight's gentle satire, *The Clinch, Movie Theatre*, exhibits the subtle humor reflected in much of her work as she suggests the irritation felt by movie-goers trying to watch a romantic scene projected on the silver screen. The American Federation of Arts selected this image for an exhibition of modern American printmaking at the Bibliothèque nationale in Paris in 1928.

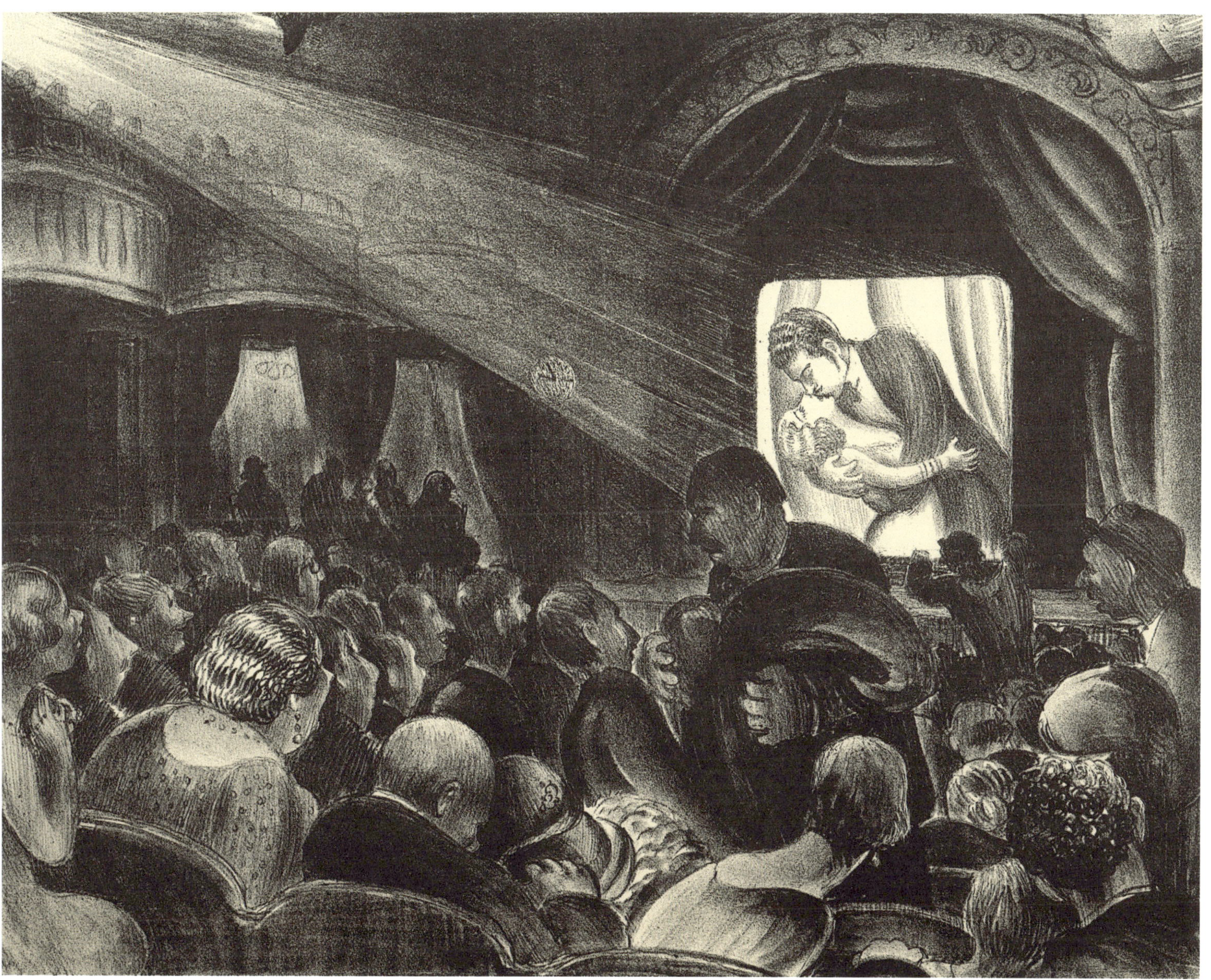

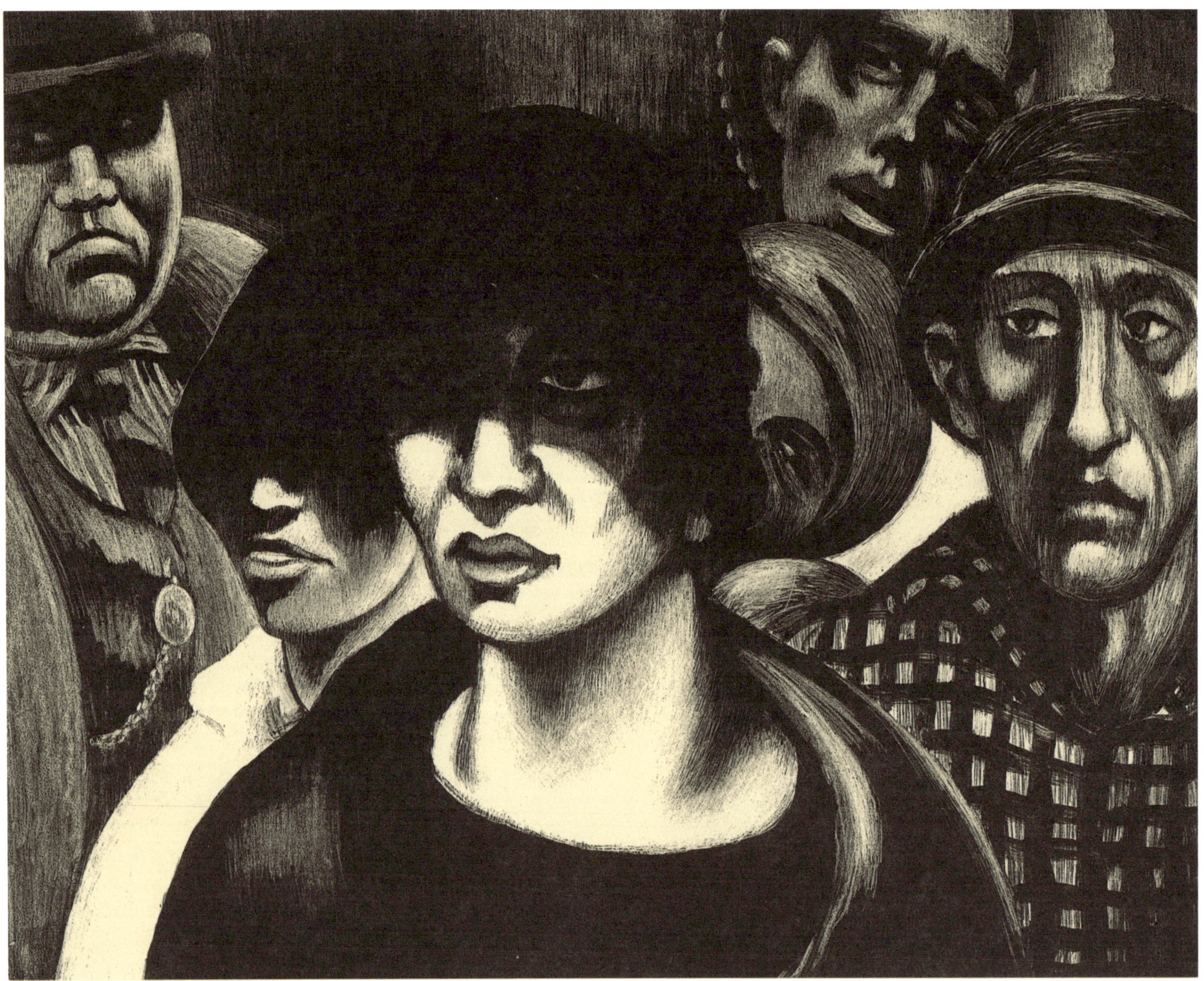

MABEL DWIGHT. *In the Crowd.*
Lithograph. 1931.

Mabel Dwight moved easily between comedy and tragedy in the lives of people she portrayed in her prints. Here, she captures despair, perhaps born of the Great Depression, in the faces of six individuals standing in a crowd.

PLATE 9
ISABEL BISHOP. *Office Girls*.
Etching. 1938.
Reproduction courtesy of
D.C. Moore Gallery, New York, New York.

Working women, unemployed men, and resting couples were among the people Isabel Bishop observed and drew from her studio overlooking Union Square in New York. Bishop later recalled that she would constantly peer out her window as she worked to ensure the veracity of her images.

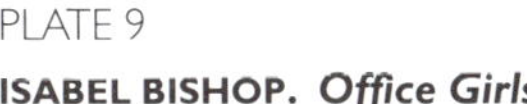

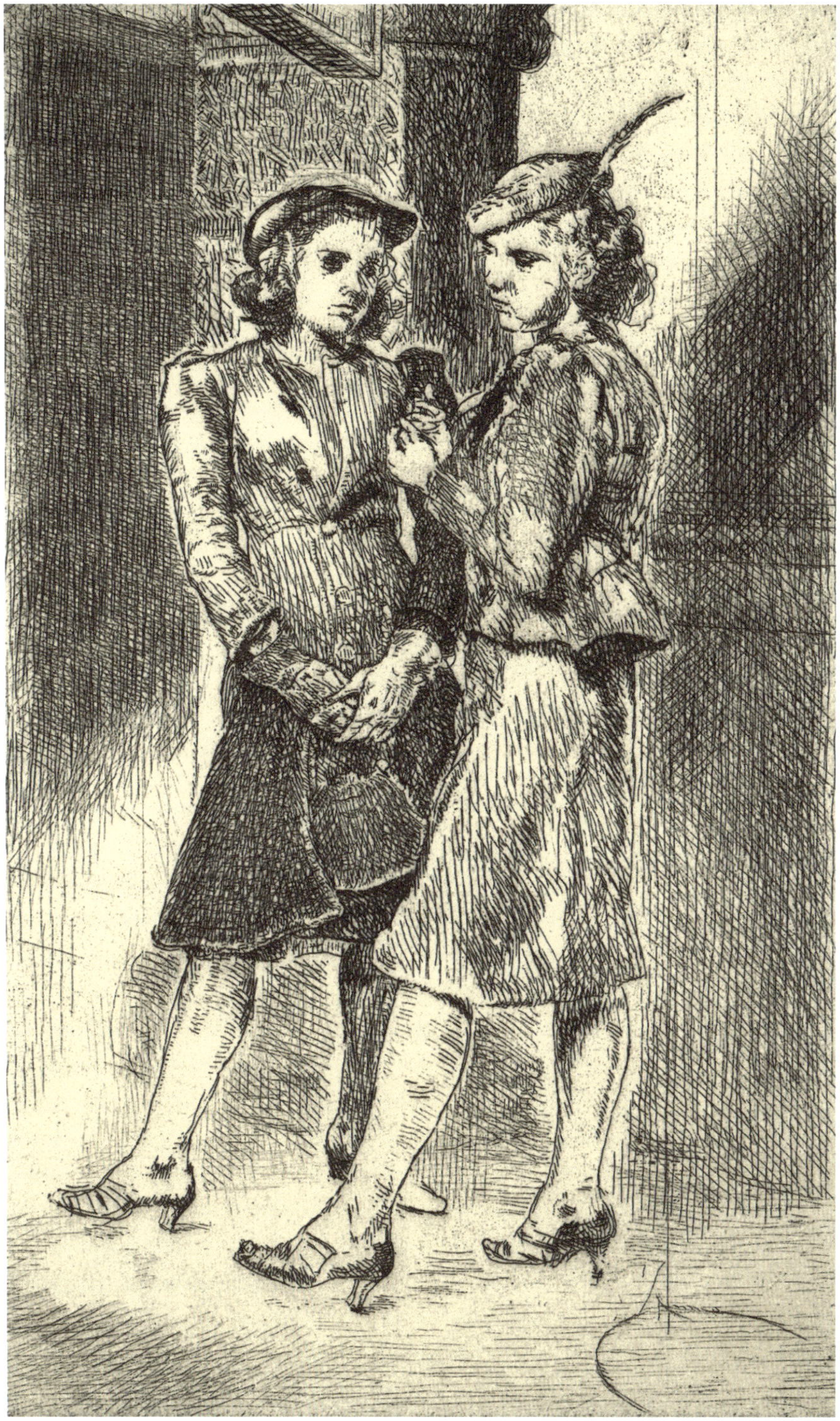

HARRY GOTTLIEB. *Going to Work.*
Screenprint. 1941.
Courtesy of Amy Gottlieb.

Harry Gottlieb achieved painterly effects with silkscreen and enjoyed the technical potential for altering the design as he worked. He used the medium in *Going to Work* to convey the dignified poverty of two workers through such narrative detail as ill-fitting clothing and shabby housing. Gottlieb's realist images rarely portrayed the worker either as a heroic figure or as someone completely broken by the effort to earn a living.

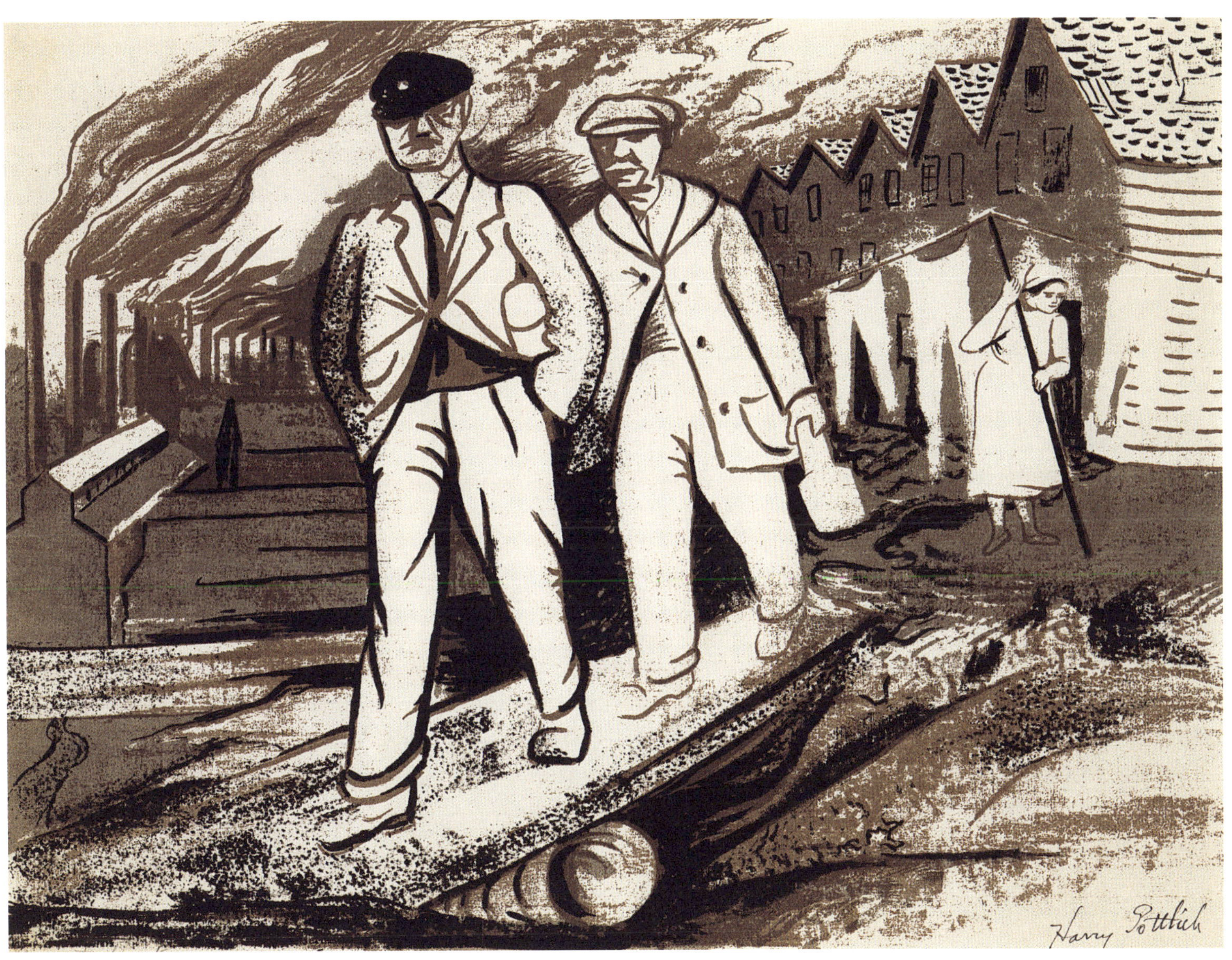

Harry Gottlieb

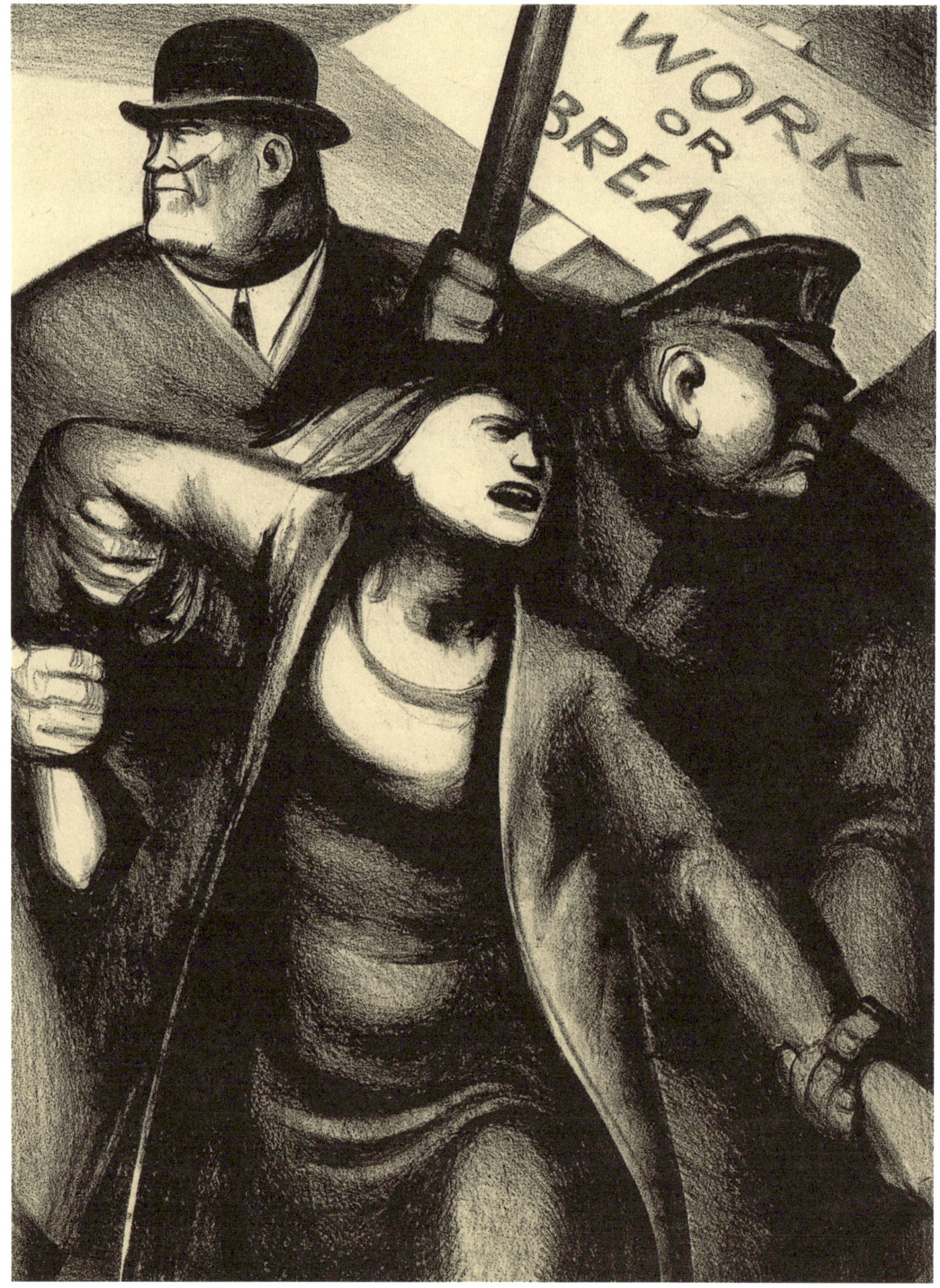

WORK
OR
BREAD

JACOB BURCK. *The Lord Provides.*
Lithograph. 1934.
Reproduction courtesy of Conrad Burck
and Joseph Burck.

With its forceful crayon strokes and strong irony,
The Lord Provides reflects Jacob Burck's training under
master political cartoonist Boardman Robinson. He
quickly absorbed Robinson's political radicalism, and
his Fourteenth Street studio became a meeting place
for leftists.

Under the auspices of the Federal Art Project,
Anton Refregier brought images of labor strife to
the public through murals created for post offices
in San Francisco and Plainfield, New Jersey. *San
Francisco '34 Waterfront Strike* is a silkscreen version
of the mural entitled *The Waterfront—1934* in the
Rincon Post Office in San Francisco, for which
Refregier received a commission in 1940 and which
he completed in 1948.

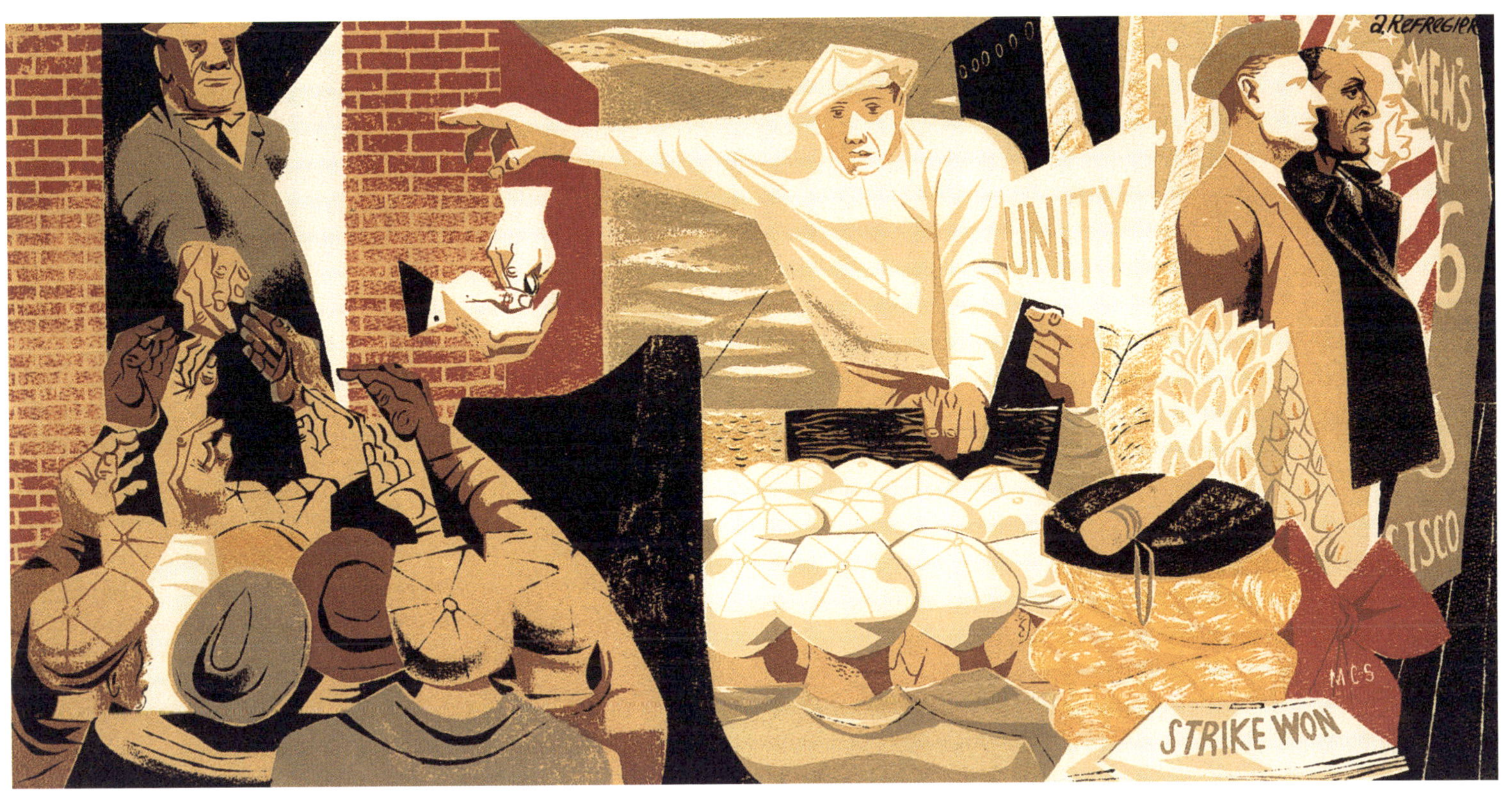
A.Refregier
UNITY
STRIKE WON
M.C.S.
ISCO
MEN'S
6

CLARE LEIGHTON. *Loading.*
Wood engraving. 1931.
Reproduction courtesy of David Leighton.

Clare Leighton helped revive the art of wood
engraving in England and America. Born in Britain in
1898, she emigrated in 1939 to the United States,
where her work had already met with success. Over
the course of a long and prolific career, she wrote
and illustrated numerous books extolling the virtues
of the American countryside and the people who
worked the land. During the 1920s and 1930s, as the
world around her became increasingly technological,
industrial, and urban, she portrayed rural working
men and women with dignity and strength in her
prints, reminding Americans of the simpler values of
hard work, fresh air, camaraderie, and community.

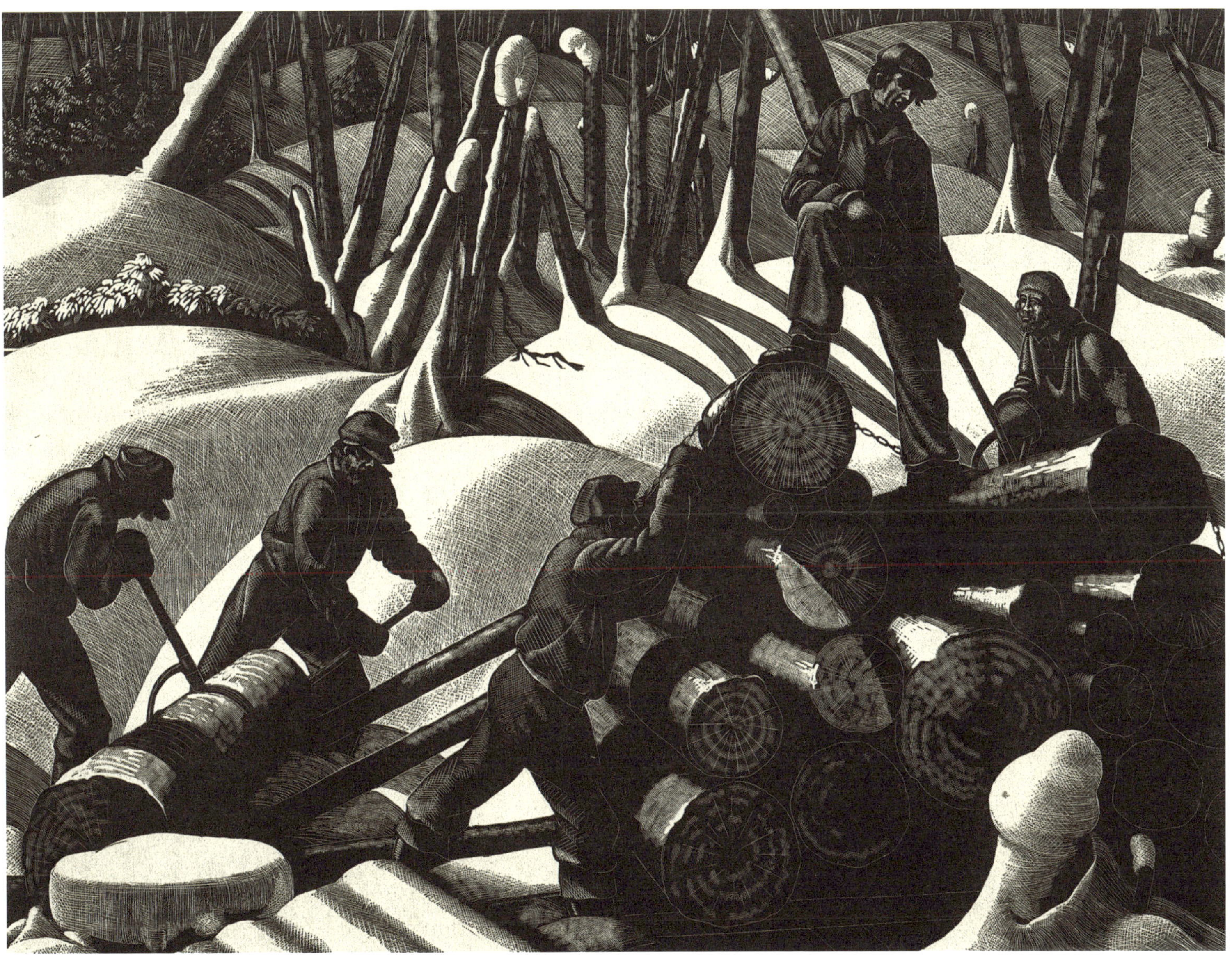

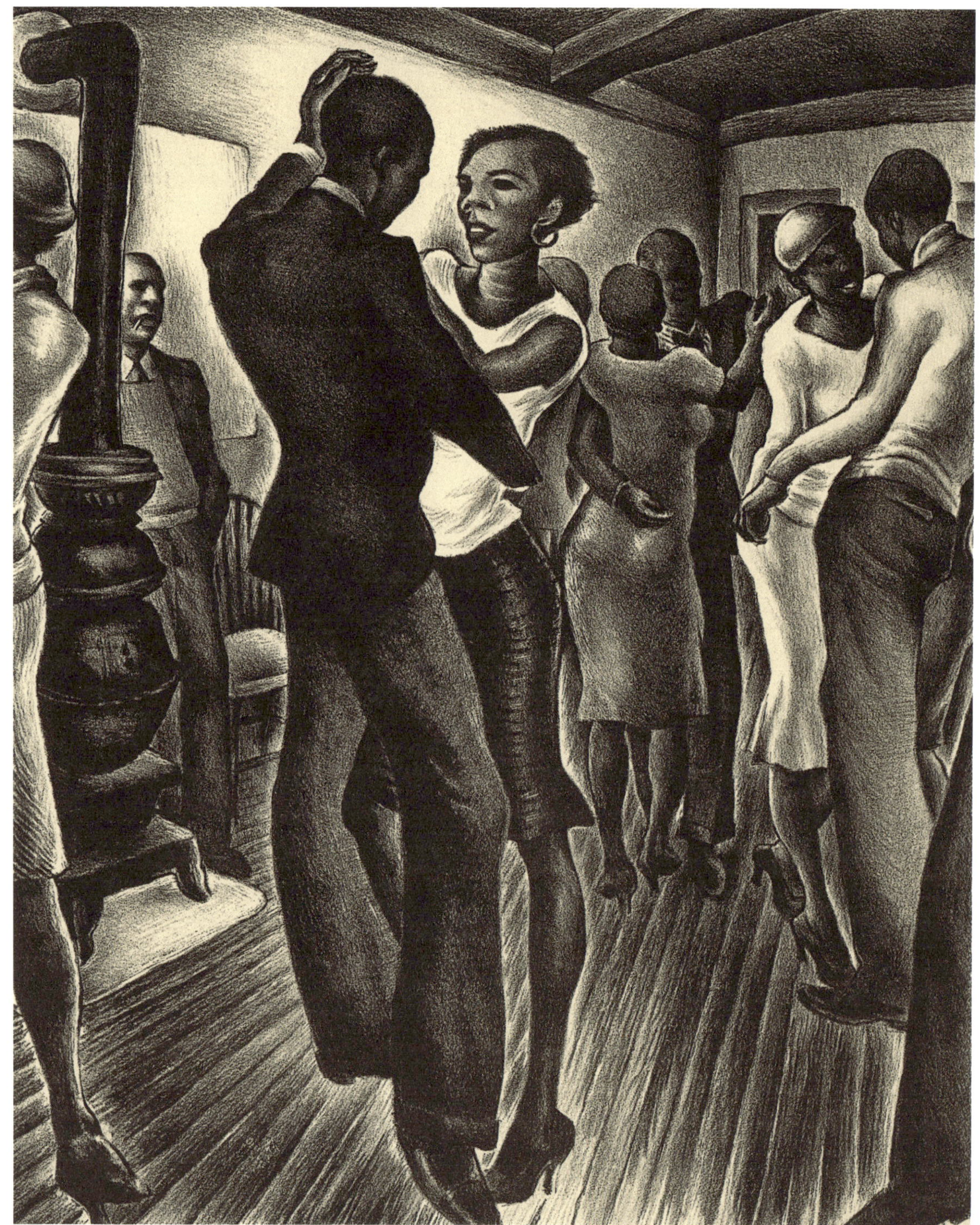

MEYER WOLFE. *Red Eye's Hall.*
Lithograph. 1934.

The lives of working class people and racial minori-
ties were of great interest to the social realists and
their largely white audience, who were drawn, for
example, to this portrayal of African Americans in a
Nashville dance hall in the 1930s.

ALBERT POTTER. *Eastside New York.*
Woodcut. Ca. 1931-35.
Reproduction courtesy of
the Estate of Albert Potter.

New York's Lower East Side was a bustling haven for
European immigrants and provided a wealth of vital
urban imagery for Potter and his fellow artists. The
humble woodcut, the earliest print format, which had
first flourished in the fifteenth century but was later
superseded by more sophisticated processes, found
new artistic life in the twentieth century when artists
like Albert Potter recognized in its crude spontaneity,
vigor, and directness an effective and appropriate
medium for graphic essays portraying the American
scene.

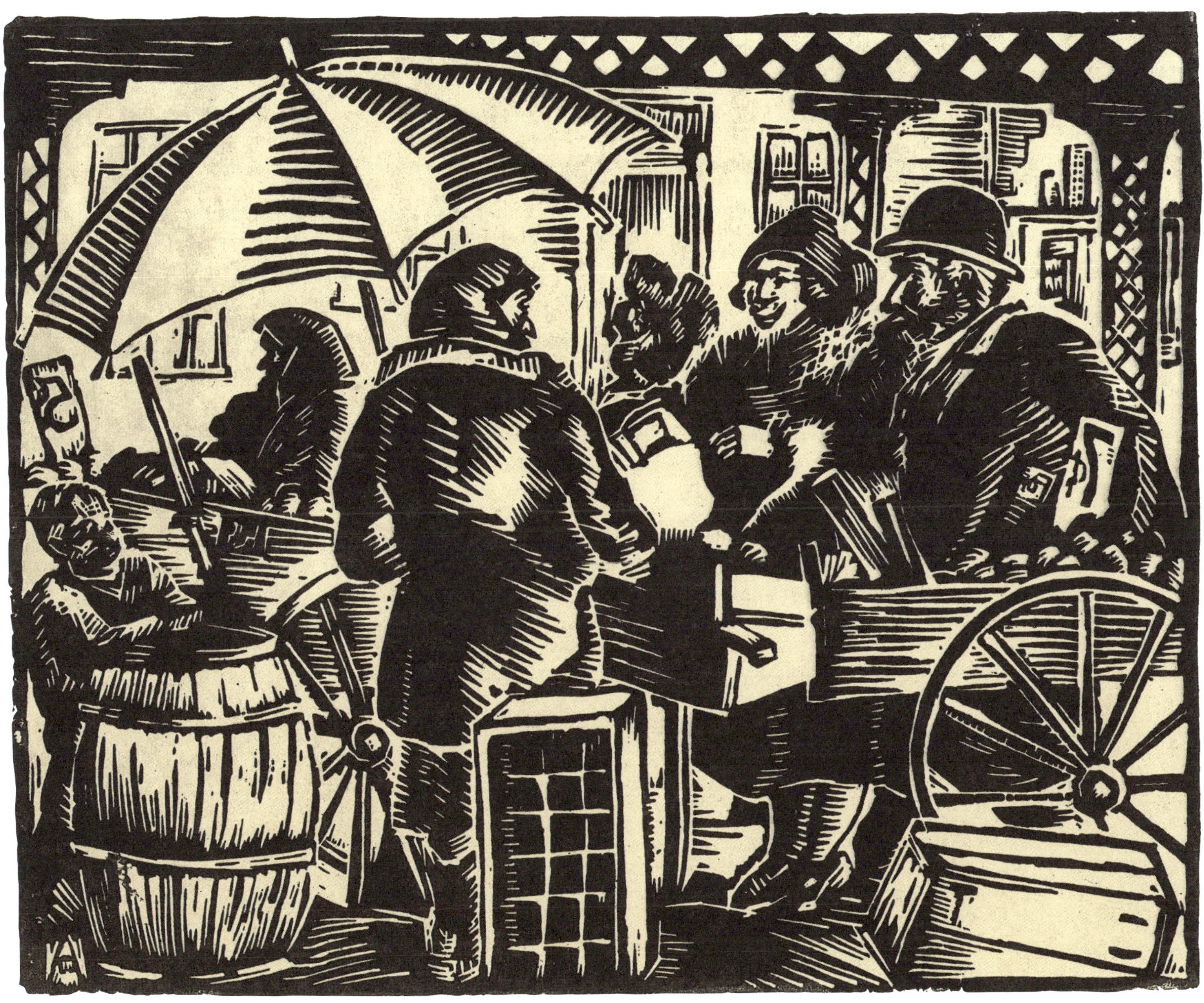

LAWRENCE BEALL SMITH. *The Skaters.*
Lithograph. 1939.
Reproduction courtesy of
the Estate of Lawrence Beall Smith.

Lawrence Beall Smith began his professional career
as a portrait painter, but a turn toward lithography
and his own imaginative rendering of the human
figure enabled him to create such animated compositions as *The Skaters*, in which he captures the spirit of
a city neighborhood and the youthful exuberance of
children in a fluid realist style.

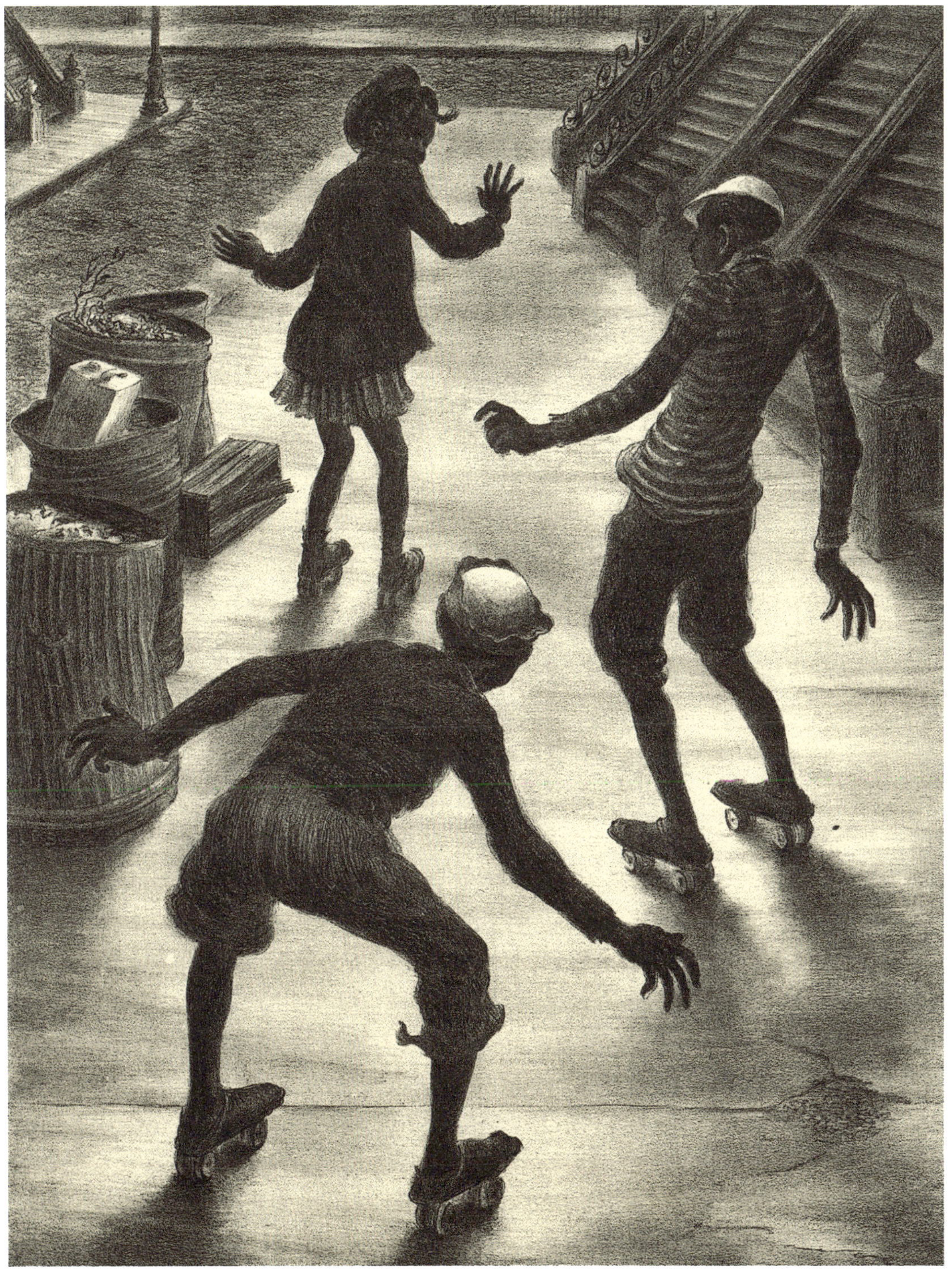

Many American artists found in Diego Rivera's political radicalism and populist imagery a model for their
own social and artistic aspirations.

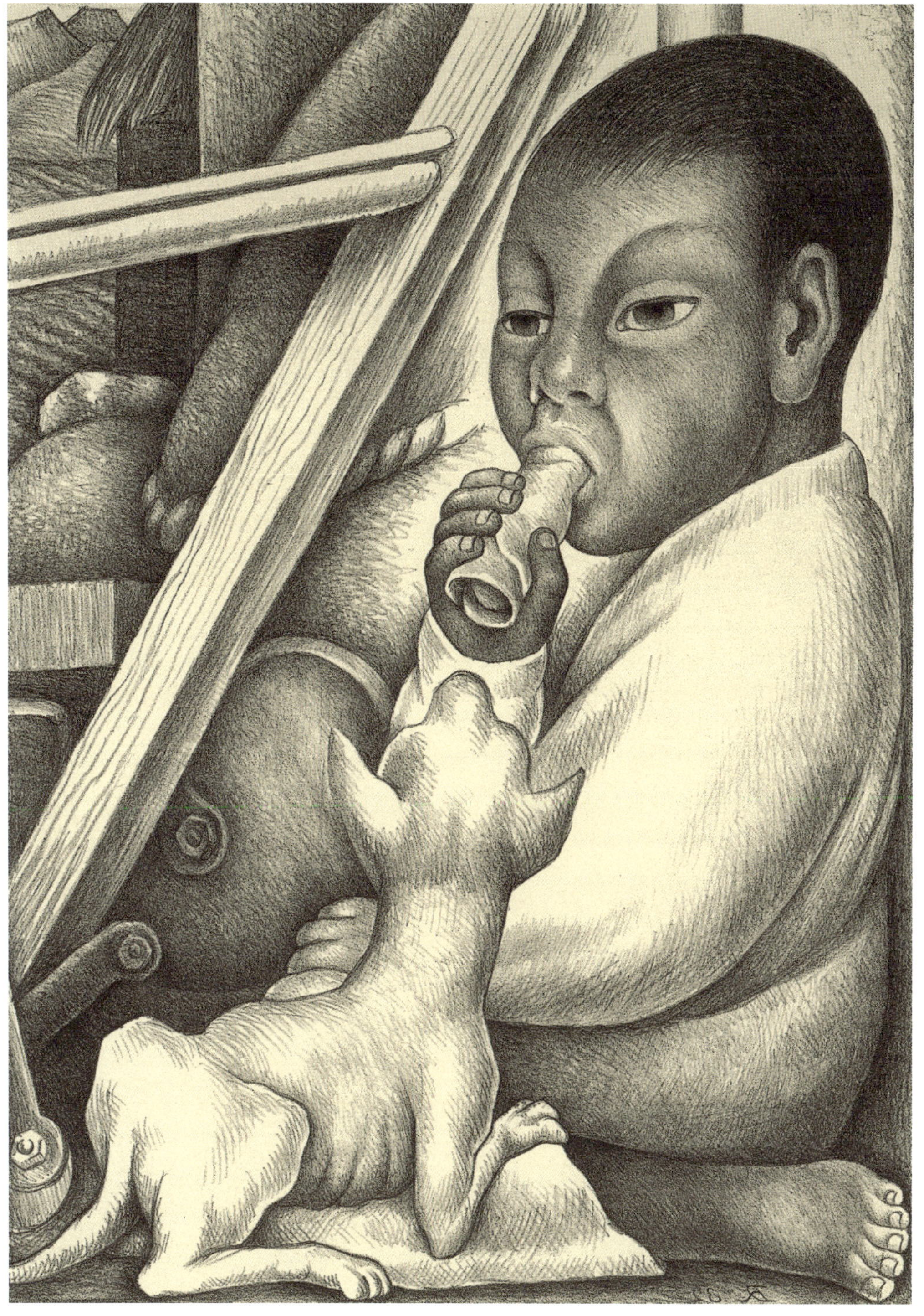

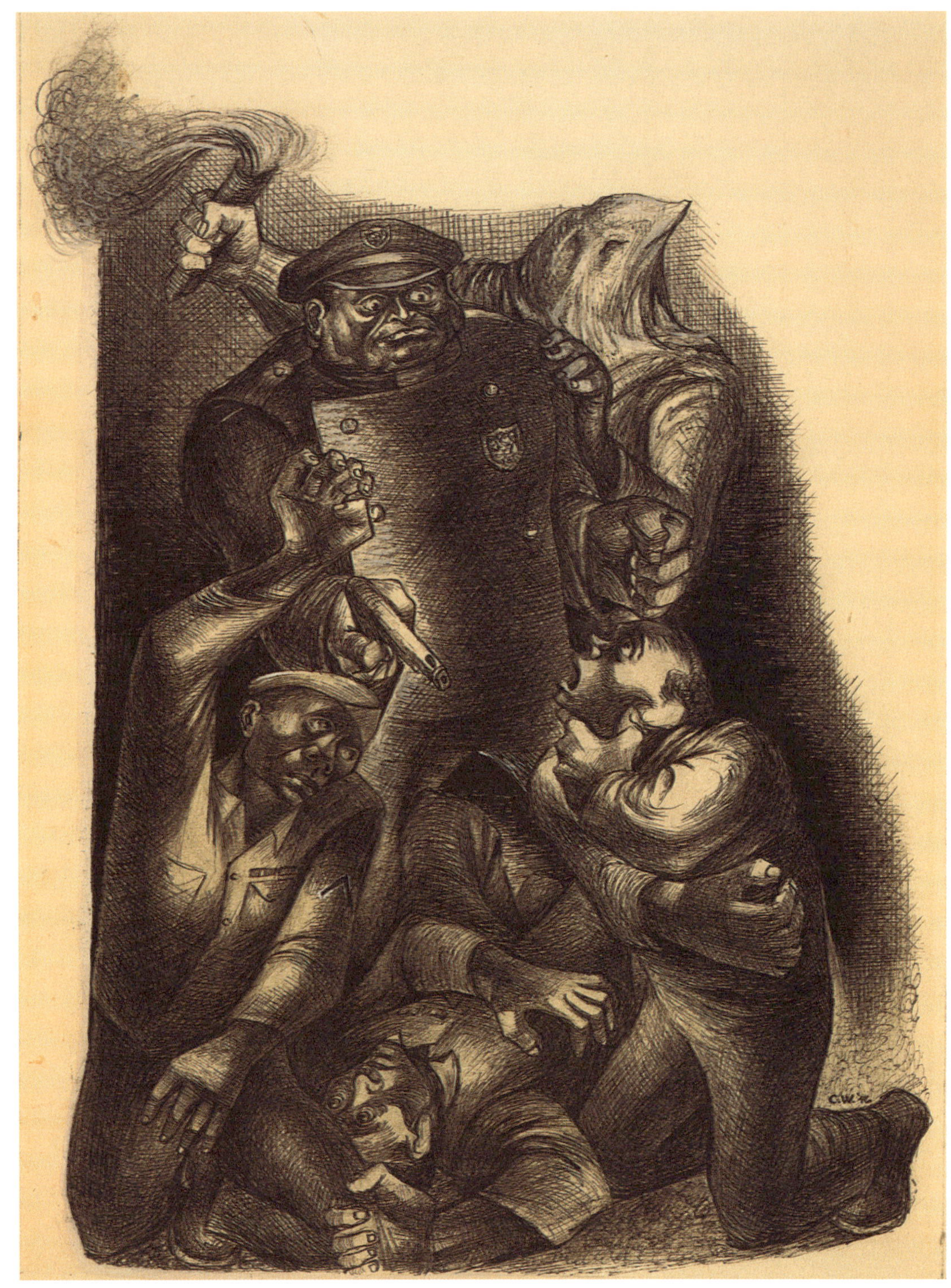

Reports of racism and violence encountered by
African American veterans of World War II as they
returned home and the artist's strong personal
commitment to social reform inspired this powerful
drawing by African American artist Charles White.
Even as a young man, White expressed his desire to
use art as a weapon to "say what I have to say" and
"fight what I resent." He probably created this image
during or shortly after his own convalescence from
tuberculosis in the Veterans Administration hospital
in Beacon, New York.

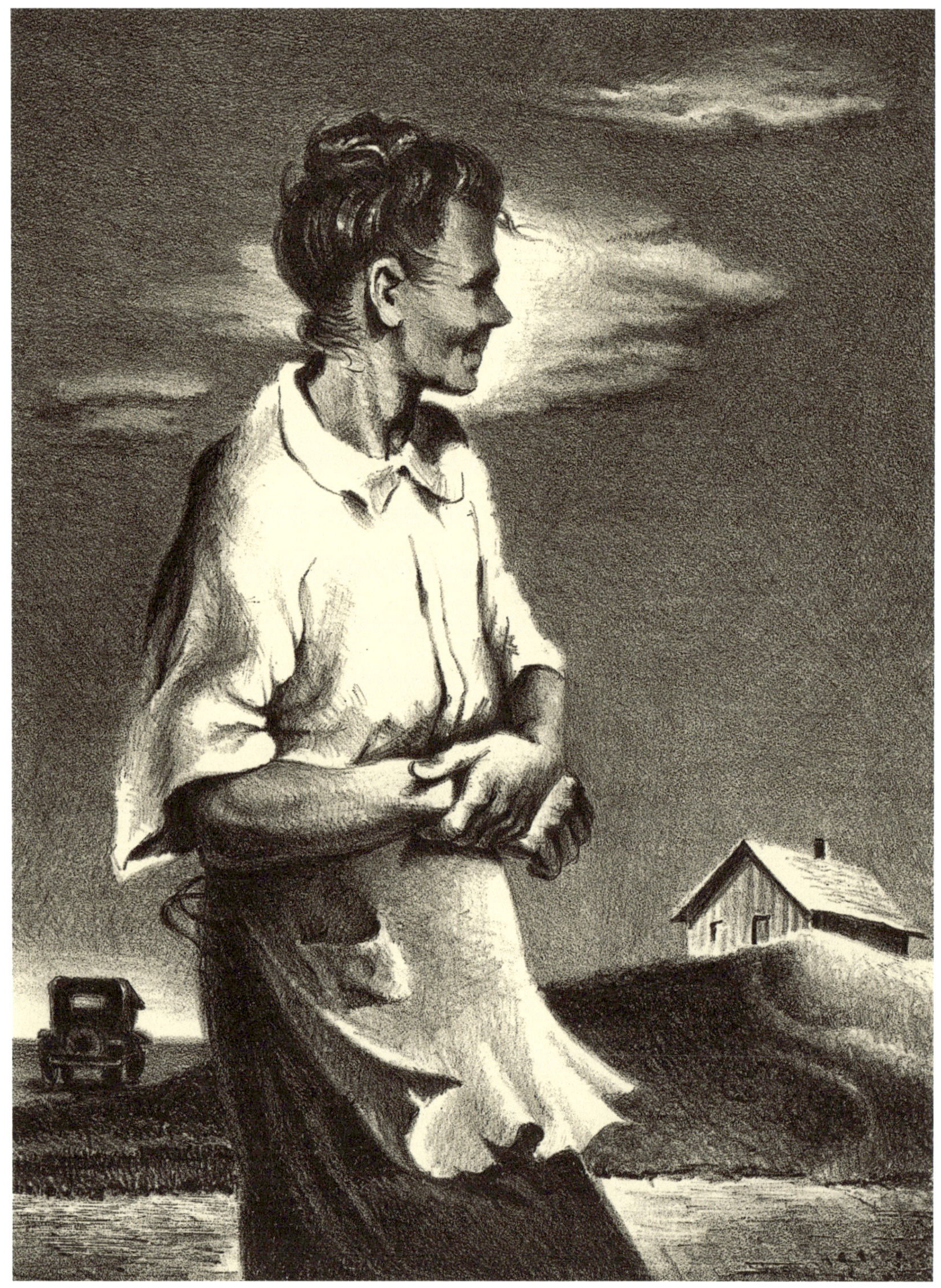

PLATE 19
GEORGES SCHREIBER. *From Arkansas.*
Lithograph. 1941.
Reproduction courtesy of
the Estate of Georges Schreiber.

The magnificent achievements of such Farm Security
Administration photographers as Walker Evans and
Dorothea Lange in documenting America and Americans during the Depression and World War II has its
graphic counterpart in the work of WPA printmakers
from the period, including Georges Schreiber, who
visited all forty-eight states while working for the
agency between 1936 and 1939.

Joseph Hirsch's father, a noted Philadelphia surgeon, posed for the sleeping figure in *Lunch Hour*, which the artist then transformed into a sensitive portrait of an African American youth. In 1944 the Library of Congress awarded this print the Second Purchase Prize, formerly known as the Pennell Prize.

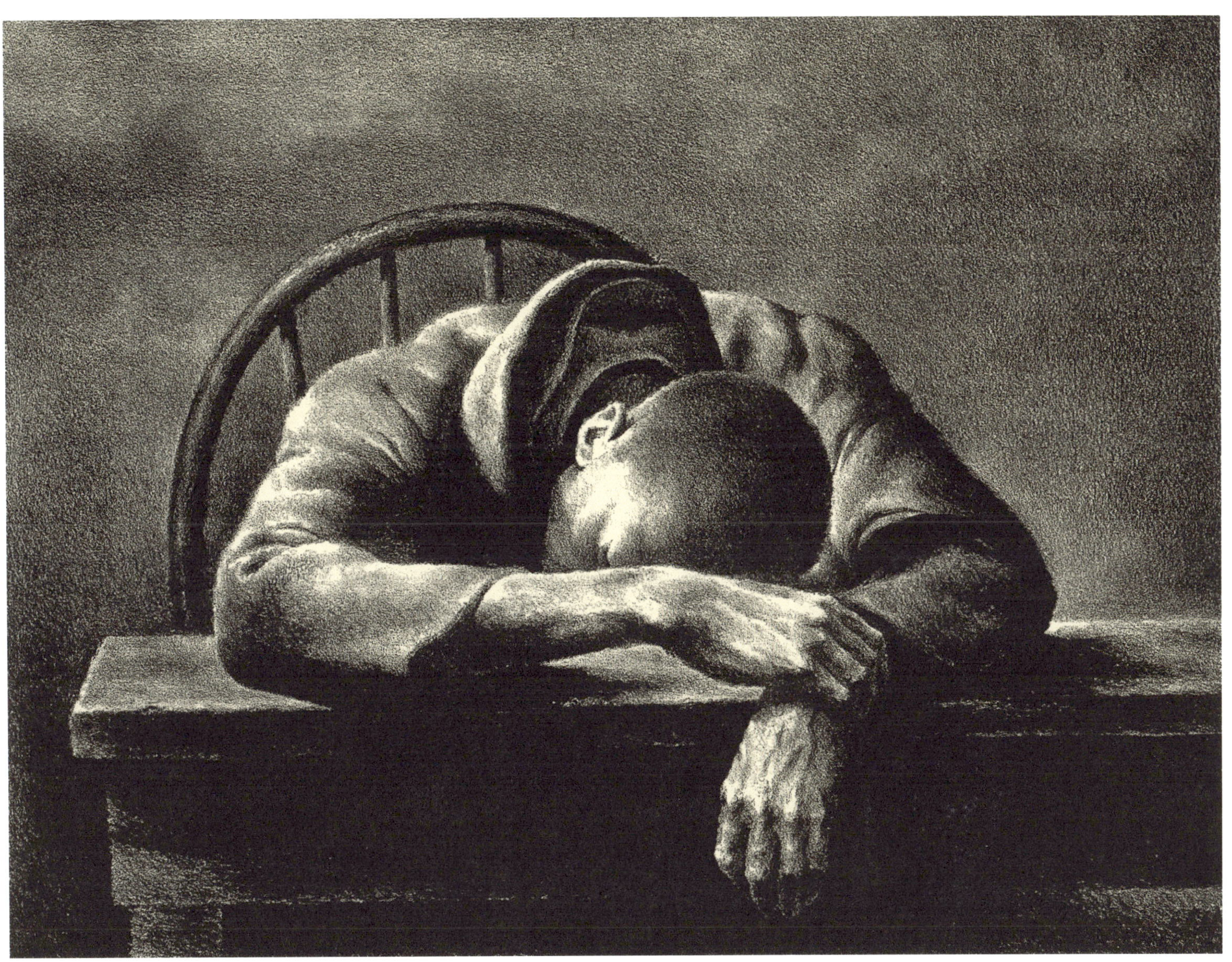

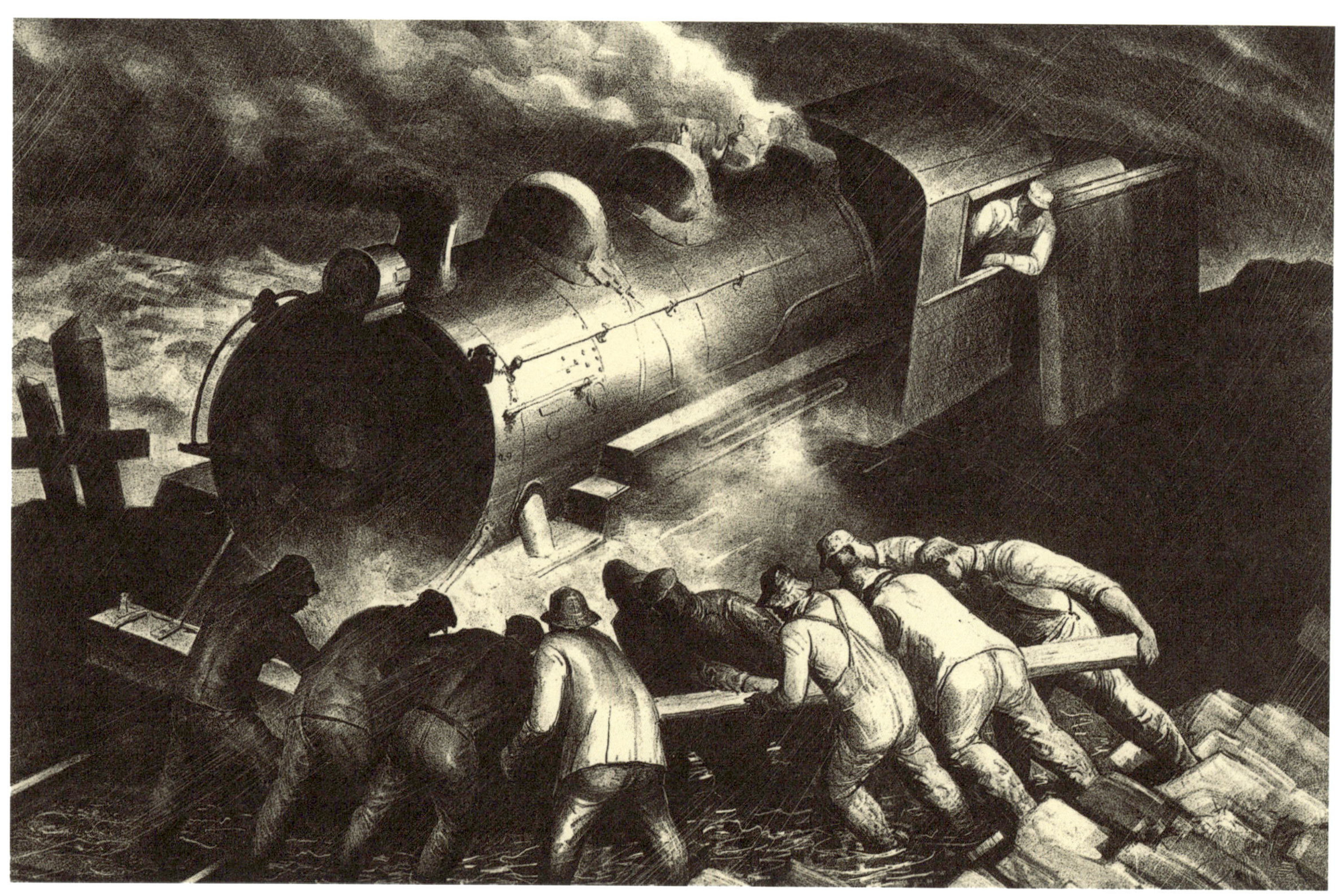

JAMES E. ALLEN 1894-1964.
Distress. 1938.
Lithograph, 9 1/16 x 14 1/8 in. (image),
10 15/16 x 15 13/16 in. (sheet);
23.1 x 35.9 cm (image), 27.8 x 40.2 cm (sheet).
Published in *Collier's*, September 17, 1938.
LC-USZC4-6581
Figure 27

PEGGY BACON 1895-1987.
Rural Retreat. 1930.
Lithograph, 11 1/8 x 15 in. (image),
13 9/16 x 17 5/8 in. (sheet);
28.2 x 38.1 cm (image), 34.4 x 44.7 cm (sheet).
LC-USZC4-6585
Figure 23

PEGGY BACON 1895-1987.
Heywood Broun. 1930.
Lithograph, 11 1/16 x 15 7/16 in. (image),
13 1/8 x 17 5/8 in. (sheet);
28 x 39.2 cm (image), 33.4 x 44.8 cm (sheet).
LC-USZC4-6600
Figure 12

LAMAR BAKER 1908-1993.
Fabric. 1940.
Lithograph, 9 5/16 x 11 13/16 in. (image),
11 5/8 x 16 1/16 in. (sheet);
23.7 x 30 cm (image), 29.5 x 40.7 cm (sheet).
LC-USZC4-6580
Figure 28

GEORGE BELLOWS 1882-1925.
In the Subway. 1921.
Lithograph, 8 1/2 x 7 1/16 in. (image),
9 1/2 x 9 3/4 in. (sheet);
21.6 x 18 cm (image), 24.2 x 24.7 cm (sheet).
Printed by Bolton Brown.
LC-USZC4-6575
Figure 10

GEORGE BELLOWS 1882-1925.
The Drunk. Ca. 1924. Second state.
Lithograph, 15 5/8 x 12 15/16 in. (image),
21 5/8 x 13 3/4 in. (sheet);
39.8 x 32.8 cm (image), 41.9 x 35 cm (sheet).
Printed by Bolton Brown.
Published as an illustration for
Mabel Potter Daggett, "Why We Prohibit,"
in *Good Housekeeping*, May 1924.
LC-USZC4-6716
PLATE 5

THOMAS HART BENTON 1889-1975.
Goin' Home. 1937.
Lithograph, 9 7/16 x 11 7/8 in. (image),
11 13/16 x 16 in. (sheet);
24 x 30.2 cm (image), 30 x 40.6 cm (sheet).
Printed by George Miller.
Distributed by Associated American Artists.
LC-USZC4-6587
Figure 3

ISABEL BISHOP 1902-1988.
Office Girls. 1938.
Etching, 7 13/16 x 4 15/16 in. (image),
12 15/16 x 9 13/16 in. (sheet);
20 x 12.5 cm (image), 32.8 x 25 cm (sheet).
LC-USZC4-6963
PLATE 9

Figure 27
JAMES E. ALLEN. *Distress.*
Lithograph. 1938.
Reproduction courtesy of
the Estate of James E. Allen.

Industrial scenes and muscular images
of men working on railroads, buildings,
and bridges form a large part of the graphic
repertoire of artist and illustrator James E.
Allen.

LUCIENNE BLOCH   1909-1999.
Diego Rivera. Ca. 1933.
Lithograph, 12 x 9 15/16 in. (image),
15 3/4 x 11 5/16 in. (sheet);
30.4 x 23.7 cm (image), 40 x 28.8 cm (sheet).
LC-USZC4-6557
Figure 15

JACOB BURCK   1907-1982.
The Lord Provides. 1934.
Lithograph, 12 x 8 7/8 in. (image),
15 3/4 x 11 1/2 in. (sheet);
30.4 x 22.5 cm (image), 40 x 29.2 cm (sheet).
Published in *The American Scene*, no. 1 (New York:
Contemporary Print Group, 1934).
LC-USZC4-6717
PLATE 11

NICOLAI CIKOVSKY   1894-1984.
On the East River. Ca. 1934
Lithograph, 11 7/8 x 15 5/16 in. (image),
15 7/8 x 22 3/4 in. (sheet);
30.1 x 38.9 cm (image), 40.3 x 57.8 cm (sheet).
LC-USZC4-6571
Figure 31

GLENN O. COLEMAN   1887-1932.
Hurdy Gurdy Ballet. 1928.
Lithograph, 12 1/8 x 15 13/16 in. (image),
15 7/8 x 22 7/8 in. (sheet);
30.8 x 40.2 cm (image), 40.3 x 58.1 cm (sheet).
LC-USZC4-6601
Figure 5

JOHN STEUART CURRY   1897-1946.
Manhunt. 1934.
Lithograph, 10 3/16 x 12 15/16 in. (image),
11 9/16 x 15 7/8 in. (sheet);
25.8 x 32.8 cm (image), 29.4 x 40.3 cm (sheet).
Published in *The American Scene*, no. 2
(New York: Contemporary Print Group, 1934).
LC-USZC4-6579
Figure 19

STUART DAVIS   1892-1964.
Hoboken. 1916.
Watercolor, 24 3/8 x 18 9/16 in. (sheet);
61.9 x 47.1 cm (sheet).
Published in the *Liberator* 1 (August 1918).
LC-USZC4-5707
LC-USZ62-119283
Figure 1

ADOLF DEHN   1895-1968.
Central Park at Night. 1934.
Lithograph, 9 7/16 x 12 11/16 in. (image),
11 7/8 x 18 13/16 in. (sheet);
24 x 32.2 cm (image), 30.1 x 47.8 cm (sheet).
Printed by George Miller.
LC-USZC4-6576
Figure 7

MABEL DWIGHT   1876-1955.
The Clinch, Movie Theatre. 1928. Second state.
Lithograph, 9 1/8 x 11 5/8 in. (image),
11 1/16 x 14 5/16 in. (sheet);
23.2 x 29.6 cm (image), 28 x 36.4 cm (sheet).
Printed by George Miller.
LC-USZC4-6573
PLATE 7

MABEL DWIGHT   1876-1955.
In the Crowd. 1931.
Lithograph, 9 7/16 x 11 3/4 in. (image),
11 x 16 in. (sheet); 24 x 29.9 cm (image),
 28 x 40.6 cm (sheet).
Printed by George Miller.
LC-USZC4-6582
PLATE 8

FRED ELLIS   1885-1965.
54 Hour Week / Low Wages. Ca. 1930s.
Crayon, ink, pencil, and opaque white;
13 13/16 x 16 3/4 in. (sheet).
35.1 x 42.6 cm (sheet).
Published in the *Daily Worker*.
LC-USZC4-6598
Figure 11

WANDA GÁG   1893-1946.
Winter Garden. 1935.
Lithograph, 10 1/16 x 8 1/4 in. (image),
16 x 12 in. (sheet);
25.5 x 21 cm (image), 40.6 x 30.5 cm (sheet).
Distributed by the American Artists Group, Inc.
LC-USZC4-6583
Figure 32

HUGO GELLERT   1892-1985.
The Working Day, no. 37. Ca. 1933.
Lithograph, 15 3/16 x 13 3/16 in. (image),
21 9/16 x 15 3/16 in. (sheet);
38.6 x 33.5 cm (image), 54.7 x 38.6 cm (sheet).
Published in *Karl Marx in Pictures*
(Paris: E. Desjobert, 1933).
LC-USZC4-6586
Figure 21

HENRY GLINTENKAMP 1887–1946.
Girls Wanted. 1916.
Crayon, 26 x 22 5/16 in. (sheet);
66 x 56.7 cm (sheet).
Published in *The Masses*, no. 8 (February 1916), p. 9.
LC-USZC4-5712
LC-USZ62-119277
PLATE 2

HARRY GOTTLIEB 1895–1992.
Going to Work. 1941.
Screenprint, 14 15/16 x 20 1/16 in. (image),
17 13/16 x 23 3/4 in. (sheet);
38 x 50.9 cm (image), 45.3 x 60.4 cm (sheet).
LC-USZC4-6715
PLATE 10

Figure 28
LAMAR BAKER. *Fabric.*
Lithograph. 1940.
Reproduction courtesy of
the Estate of Lamar Baker.

Graphic arts historian and curator Carl
Zigrosser considered Lamar Baker "one of
the first native artists to reckon with the
problems of the new South." Baker's portfolio of lithographs entitled the *Cotton Series*,
which includes *Fabric*, combines mysticism,
magic, and symbolic imagery of cotton
production with compassion for the share-
cropper's daily struggle for dignity and
subsistence.

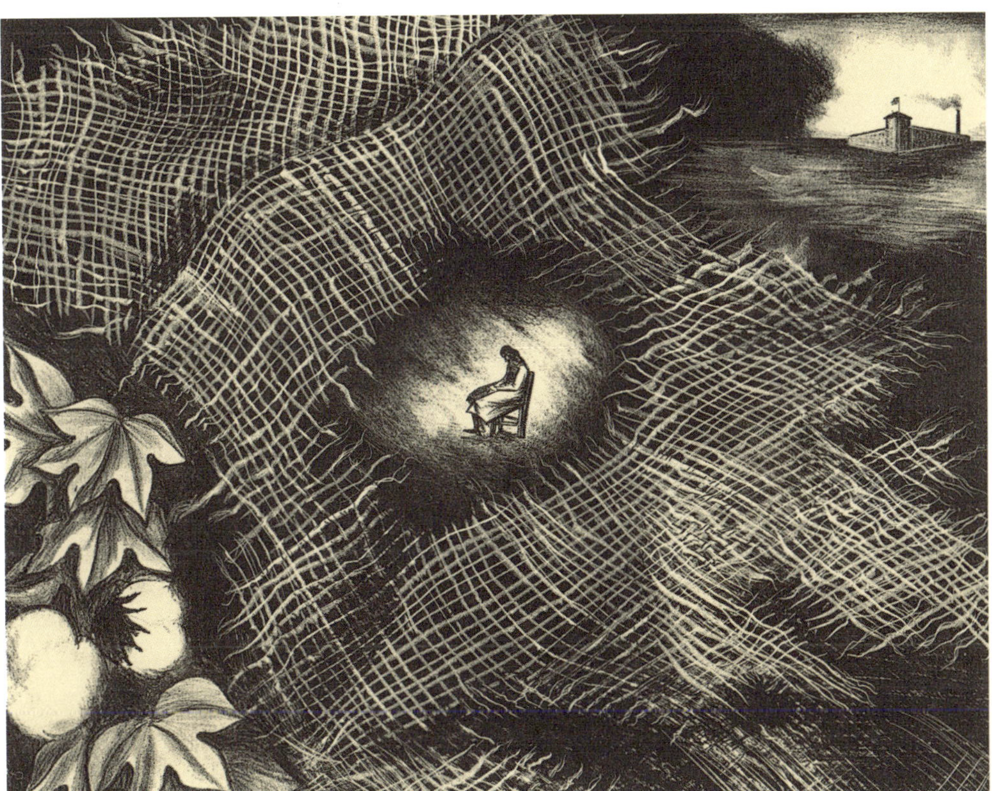

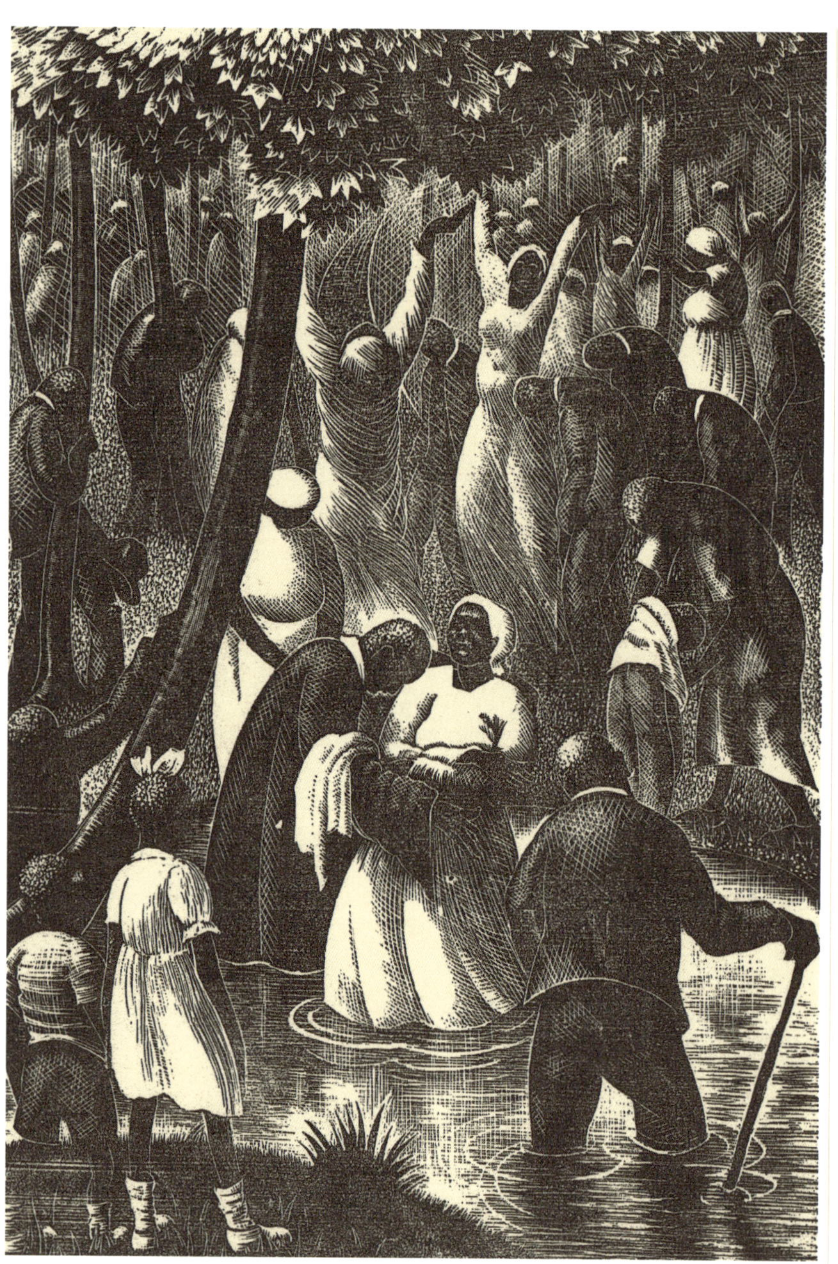

BLANCHE GRAMBS born 1916.
No Work. 1935.
Lithograph, 9 7/16 × 8 1/16 in. (image),
15 15/16 × 11 7/16 in. (sheet);
24 × 20.5 cm (image), 40.5 × 29 cm (sheet).
Printed at the Art Students League by Will Barnet.
LC-USZC4-6574
Figure 4

WILLIAM GROPPER 1897-1977.
***The Troublemaker Who Acts Like a Provocateur
at the Caucus.*** 1943.
Ink and white with spatter,
16 3/4 × 10 7/16 in. (sheet);
42.6 × 26.5 cm (sheet).
Illustration for *Avreml Broide*, by Ben Gold
(New York: Prompt Press, 1944), 138.
LC-USZC4-6595
Figure 13

Figure 29
CLARE LEIGHTON. *The Baptism.*
Wood engraving. Ca. 1948.
Reproduction courtesy of David Leighton.

Clare Leighton's wood engraving *The
Baptism*, or *The Baptizing*, illustrates text concerning folk beliefs about childhood in the
first volume of *The Frank C. Brown Collection
of North Carolina Folklore* (Durham: Duke
University Press, 1952). The artist received a
commission to illustrate the seven-volume
series while she was visiting lecturer in art at
Duke University in 1943-44. She visited the
North Carolina mountains on a research trip
in 1946, completing illustrations for the
entire series by December 1950.

ROBERT GWATHMEY 1903-1988.
Non Fiction. 1945.
Screenprint, 17 1/8 x 13 7/8 in. (image),
23 1/2 x 16 15/16 in. (sheet);
43.5 x 35.3 cm (image), 59.7 x 43.1 cm (sheet).
LC-USZC4-6577
PLATE 1

JOSEPH HIRSCH 1910-1981.
Lunch Hour. 1942.
Lithograph, 9 x 11 7/8 in. (image),
11 1/8 x 14 3/16 in. (sheet);
22.8 x 30.1 cm (image), 28.2 x 36.1 cm (sheet).
Distributed by Associated American Artists.
Printed by George Miller.
LC-USZC4-6718
PLATE 20

VICTORIA HUTSON HUNTLEY 1900-1971.
Koppers Coke. 1932.
Lithograph, 9 5/8 x 13 3/8 in. (image),
13 3/4 x 17 7/16 in. (sheet);
24.5 x 34 cm (image), 34.9 x 44.3 cm (sheet).
LC-USZC4-6578
Figure 40

JOE JONES 1909-1963.
Wastelands. 1937.
Lithograph, 9 15/16 x 11 13/16 in. (image),
12 1/2 x 17 15/16 in. (sheet);
25.2 x 30 cm (image), 31.7 x 45.6 cm (sheet).
Distributed by the American Artists Group.
LC-USZC4-6603
Figure 20

SAUL KOVNER 1904-1981.
Small Town Harlem. 1940.
Lithograph, 10 7/16 x 14 1/8 in. (image),
13 7/16 x 16 1/16 in. (sheet);
28.7 x 35.9 cm (image), 34.1 x 40.7 cm (sheet).
Stamped: New York City WPA Art Project.
LC-USZC4-6563
Figure 18

CLARE LEIGHTON 1898-1989.
The Baptism. Ca. 1948.
Wood engraving, 7 1/16 x 4 13/16 in. (image),
8 11/16 x 6 11/16 in. (sheet);
18 x 12.3 cm (image), 22 x 17 cm (sheet).
Published in *The Frank C. Brown Collection
of North Carolina Folklore*, vol. 1
(Durham, N.C.: Duke University Press, 1952),
facing p. 226.
LC-USZC4-6590
Figure 29

CLARE LEIGHTON 1898-1989.
Loading. 1931.
Wood engraving, 8 15/16 x 12 11/16 in. (image),
10 3/4 x 13 11/16 in. (sheet);
22.7 x 32.2 cm (image), 27.3 x 34.8 cm (sheet).
LC-USZC4-6602
PLATE 13

MICHAEL LENSON 1903-1971.
*Full Production and Full Employment under
Our Democratic System of Private Enterprise.*
Ca. 1944.
Crayon and ink, 19 5/16 x 24 in. (sheet);
49 x 61 cm (sheet).
LC-USZC4-6568
Figure 22

MARTIN LEWIS 1881-1962.
Boss of the Block. Ca. 1939.
Aquatint and etching, 11 1/8 x 7 3/8 in. (image),
16 1/16 x 10 15/16 in. (sheet);
28.2 x 18.8 cm (image), 40.8 x 27.8 cm (sheet).
LC-USZC4-6713
Figure 14

LOUIS LOZOWICK 1892-1973.
Guts of Manhattan. 1939.
Lithograph, 13 3/16 x 9 5/16 in. (image),
16 x 10 5/8 in. (sheet);
33.5 x 23.6 cm (image), 40.6 x 27 (sheet).
Printed by George Miller.
LC-USZC4-6572
Figure 26

KYRA MARKHAM 1891-1967.
Flag Raising in Leroy St. 1942.
Lithograph, 13 1/16 x 9 11/16 in. (image),
15 13/16 x 11 in. (sheet);
33.1 x 24.6 cm (image), 40.2 x 28 cm (sheet).
LC-USZC4-6589
Figure 25

ROBERT MINOR 1884-1952.
Morgan, Mellon, and Rockefeller. Ca. 1922.
Crayon and ink, 12 5/8 x 7 in. (sheet);
32 x 17.8 cm (sheet).
LC-USZC4-5709
LC-USZ62-119275
PLATE 3

ROBERT MINOR 1884-1952.
Pittsburgh. 1916.
Lithographic crayon and India ink,
20 1/16 × 25 9/16 in. (sheet);
50.9 × 65 cm (sheet).
Published in *The Masses*, no. 8 (August 1916).
LC-USZ62-111306
LC-USZC4-4903
Figure 8

M. LOIS MURPHY 1901-1962.
"Weighing Fish" 1936-37.
Wood engraving, 7 × 9 in. (image),
8 11/16 × 11 1/8 in. (sheet);
17.8 × 22.8 cm (image), 22 × 28.3 (sheet).
LC-USZC4-6584
Figure 33

PABLO O'HIGGINS 1904-1983.
Papelero en el zocalo. 1943.
Lithograph, 15 1/4 × 19 5/16 in. (image),
17 11/16 × 23 1/4 in. (sheet);
38.8 × 49 cm (image), 44.9 × 59 cm (sheet).
LC-USZC4-6594
Figure 30

ELIZABETH OLDS 1896-1991.
White Collar Boys. 1936.
Lithograph, 11 1/8 × 14 15/16 in. (image),
13 3/4 × 18 11/16 in. (sheet);
28.2 × 37.9 cm (image), 35 × 47.5 cm (sheet).
LC-USZC4-6566
Figure 24

ELIZABETH OLDS 1896-1991.
Miner Joe. 1940.
Screenprint, 24 × 18 1/4 in. (image),
24 × 19 in. (sheet);
61 × 46.3 cm (image), 61 × 48.3 cm (sheet).
LC-USZC4-6599
PLATE 4

JOSÉ CLEMENTE OROZCO 1883-1949.
Mujer mexicana. 1929.
Lithograph, 13 15/16 × 9 15/16 in. (image),
22 11/16 × 16 in. (sheet);
35.4 × 25.3 cm (image), 57.7 × 40.6 cm (sheet).
LC-USZC4-6591
Figure 34

JAMES PENNEY 1910-1982.
Columbus Circle. 1932.
Lithograph, 11 1/4 × 15 1/4 in. (image),
12 5/16 × 18 15/16 in. (sheet);
28.5 × 38.7 cm (image), 31.3 × 48.1 cm (sheet).
LC-USZC4-6565
Figure 39

ALBERT POTTER 1903-1937.
Eastside New York. Ca. 1931–35.
Woodcut, 8 1/16 × 10 1/16 in. (image),
9 1/8 × 12 1/8 in. (sheet).
20.5 × 25.6 cm (image), 23.2 × 30.8 cm (sheet).
LC-USZC4-6596
PLATE 15

ANTON REFREGIER 1905-1979.
San Francisco '34 Waterfront Strike.
Between 1940 and 1948.
Screenprint, 11 5/16 × 21 5/16 in. (image),
18 1/4 × 27 3/16 in. (sheet);
28.8 × 55.8 cm (image), 46.4 × 69.1 cm (sheet).
LC-USZC4-6564
PLATE 12

DIEGO RIVERA 1886-1957.
Niño con taco. 1932.
Lithograph, 16 1/2 × 12 5/8 in. (image),
21 5/8 × 15 15/16 in. (sheet);
41.9 × 32 cm (image), 55 × 40.5 cm (sheet).
LC-USZC4-6570
PLATE 17

JAMES N. ROSENBERG 1874-1970.
Oct 29 Dies Irae. 1929.
Lithograph, 13 5/8 × 10 7/16 in. (image),
15 15/16 × 11 1/2 in. (sheet);
34.6 × 26.5 cm (image), 40.5 × 28.7 cm (sheet).
Printed by George Miller
LC-USZC4-4893
PLATE 6

GEORGES SCHREIBER 1904-1977.
From Arkansas. 1941.
Lithograph, 12 5/8 × 9 15/16 in. (image),
16 1/16 × 10 15/16 in. (sheet);
32 × 23.7 cm (image), 40.7 × 27.8 cm (sheet).
Distributed by Associated American Artists.
LC-USZC4-6562
PLATE 19

JOHN SLOAN 1871-1951.
"Tee Hee" Boys: Born with a Vote and a Partial Sense of the Ridiculous. 1912.
Ink and crayon, 8 9/16 x 10 3/16 in. (sheet),
10 3/4 x 13 3/8 in. (board);
21.8 x 25.8 cm (sheet), 27.3 x 34 cm (board).
Published in *Collier's* (May 18, 1912),
as: "Aw, Susie, be them dishes washed?"
LC-USZC4-5708
LC-USZ62-119292
Figure 9

LAWRENCE BEALL SMITH 1909-1995.
The Skaters. 1939.
Lithograph, 11 1/4 x 8 7/8 in. (image),
15 7/16 x 11 11/16 in. (sheet);
28.5 x 22 cm (image), 39.2 x 30.2 cm (sheet).
LC-USZC4-6561
PLATE 16

MOSES SOYER 1899-1974.
Defense Workers. 1942-43.
Lithograph, 10 3/16 x 14 15/16 in. (image),
16 3/16 x 20 13/16 in. (sheet);
25.8 x 38 cm (image), 41.1 x 52.8 cm (sheet).
LC-USZC4-6597
Figure 16

RAPHAEL SOYER 1899-1987.
Waterfront. 1934.
Lithograph, 9 x 13 3/8 in. (image),
11 3/8 x 15 13/16 in. (sheet);
22.8 x 34 cm (image), 28.9 x 40.1 cm (sheet).
Published in *The American Scene*
(New York: Contemporary Print Group, 1934).
LC-USZC4-6560
Figure 35

BERNARD JOSEPH STEFFEN 1907-1980.
Dusty Plowing. 1939.
Lithograph, 8 9/16 x 11 5/8 in. (image),
11 1/2 x 15 7/8 in. (sheet).
21.8 x 29.6 cm (image), 29.2 x 40.4 cm (sheet).
Stamped: New York City WPA Art Project.
LC-USZC4-6559
Figure 17

HARRY STERNBERG born 1904.
Builders. 1935-36.
Lithograph, 13 in. diameter (image),
9 5/8 x 15 3/4 in. (sheet);
33 cm diameter (image), 49.8 x 40 cm (sheet).
Stamped left margin: Federal Art Project WPA NYC.
LC-USZC4-6719
Figure 2

PRENTISS TAYLOR 1907-1991.
Assembly Church. 1936.
Lithograph, 9 1/2 x 13 1/4 in. (image),
12 x 17 15/16 in. (sheet);
24.2 x 33.6 cm (image), 30.4 x 45.6 cm (sheet).
LC-USZC4-6592
Figure 36

CHARLES WHITE 1918-1979.
The Return of the Soldier. 1946.
Pen and ink, 24 1/4 x 18 7/8 in. (sheet).
61.6 x 47.9 cm (sheet).
LC-USZC4-4886
PLATE 18

ELIZABETH WHITE 1893-1976.
All God's Chillun' Got Wings! Ca. 1933
Soft-ground etching and aquatint,
11 x 6 15/16 in. (image), 13 7/8 x 8 13/16 in. (sheet);
27.9 x 17.7 cm (image), 35.3 x 22.4 cm (sheet).
LC-USZC4-6164
Figure 37

MEYER WOLFE 1897-1985.
Tuesday—Othelia. 1934.
Lithograph, 11 1/8 x 14 1/16 in. (image),
16 1/16 x 19 1/8 in. (sheet);
28.3 x 35.7 cm (image), 40.7 x 48.5 (sheet).
LC-USZC4-6593
Figure 38

MEYER WOLFE 1897-1985.
Red Eye's Hall. 1934.
Lithograph, 14 1/2 x 11 9/16 in. (image),
18 5/8 x 15 7/16 in. (sheet);
36.8 x 29.1 cm (image), 47.3 x 39.2 cm (sheet).
LC-USZC4-6558
PLATE 14

NOTE: The checklist provides Library of Congress reproduction numbers (LC-USZC4-**** for color and LC-USZ62-**** for black-and-white photographs) for convenience in ordering copies from the Library's Photoduplication Service. Some works in this publication are protected by copyright. Before publishing images from this book, first seek appropriate copyright permissions.

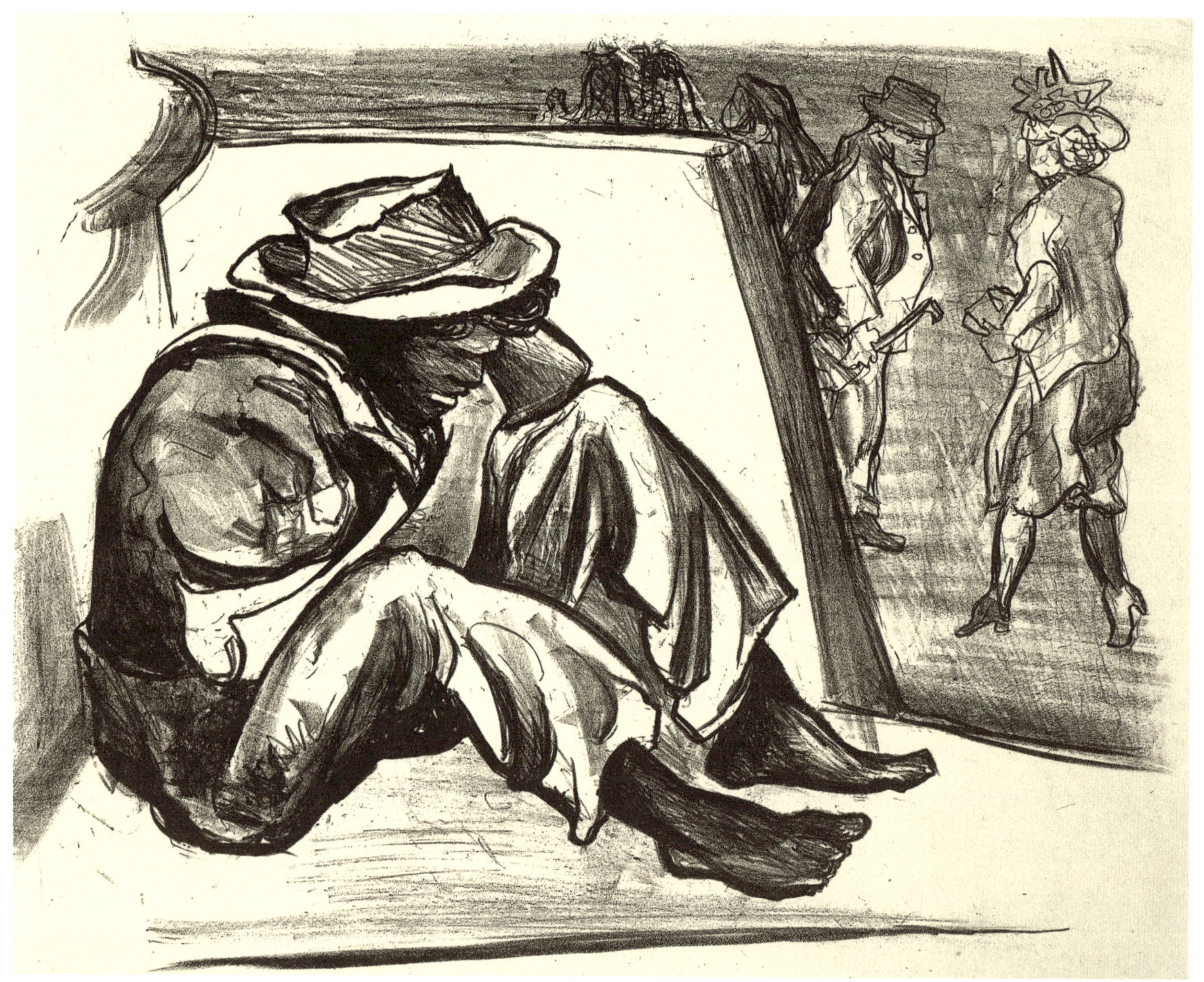

Figure 30
PABLO O'HIGGINS.
Papelero en el zocalo.
Lithograph. 1943.
Courtesy Fundacion Cultural Maria y
Pablo O'Higgins, A.C.

American-born Pablo O'Higgins worked as
an apprentice to Diego Rivera between
1924 and 1928 and was a founding member
of the internationally influential Mexican
printmakers collaborative Taller de Gráfica
Popular.

JAMES E. ALLEN, 1894-1964

Born in Missouri, James Allen worked as a magazine illustrator, traveling to Paris in 1925, where he
shared a studio with fellow printmaker Howard
Cook. There Allen experimented with various
artistic media, making lithographs and etchings for
the first time. Forced by the Depression to
return to the United States, he moved to New
York, continuing to hone his skills as a printmaker
under Joseph Pennell and William Auerbach-Levy.
The commissions he received from businesses
and magazines provided the major impetus for
his work. A dedicated and meticulous printmaker,
Allen often created lithographs rather than
drawings for reproduction. In 1943, he stopped
making prints and focused instead on painting in a
modernist style.

"Etchings and Lithographs of Industrial Subjects Make Fine
Show." *Washington Star*, March 6, 1938.

*Graphic Excursions—American Prints in Black and White,
1900-1950: Selections from the Collection of Reba and Dave
Williams*, p. 138. Essays by Karen F. Beall and David W. Kiehl.
Boston: D.R. Godine in association with the American Federation of Arts, 1991.

James E. Allen. New York: Mary Ryan Gallery, [ca. 1984].

North, Bill, and Stephen H. Goddard. *Rural America: Prints
from the Collection of Steven Schmidt*, p. 36. Lawrence:
Spencer Museum of Art, University of Kansas, 1993.

PEGGY BACON, 1895-1987

Born Margaret Frances Bacon in Ridgefield,
Connecticut, Peggy Bacon attended the School of
Applied Arts for Women in New York City in
1913 and studied landscape painting with Jonas
Lie on Long Island in 1914. From 1915 until 1920
she studied at the Art Students League, where

she came under the influence of instructors Kenneth Hayes Miller and John Sloan. The work of
Honoré Daumier inspired her interest in caricature and satire, and in 1928 she learned the art of
lithography. Besides making satirical prints, she
wrote children's books and one adult mystery,
painted, and did embroidery. By 1955 she had
ceased printmaking and turned exclusively to
painting. Even in this medium, her wry sense of
humor remained evident in her work.

Peggy Bacon: Personalities and Places. Washington: Smithsonian Institution Press, 1975.

LAMAR BAKER, 1908-1993

Lamar Baker left his native Atlanta in 1935 to
attend Harry Sternberg's classes at the Art
Students League in New York. While in New York
he completed his largest body of prints, the
so-called *Cotton Series*, consisting of twelve lithographs of which *Fabric* is one. In 1942, Baker
received a Rosenwald Fund Fellowship that permitted him to travel and paint in the Mississippi
Delta and the Gulf Coast, taking him further into
the Deep South than his native Georgia. Baker
returned to Georgia in the 1950s, where he
continued to create images condemning social
injustice during the civil rights era.

Lamar Baker. New York: Weyhe Gallery, [n.d.]

Laufer, Marilyn. "An Awakening of Social Consciousness:
The Prints of Lamar Baker." *Art Papers* 20 (May / June
1996):64.

*Nobody Knows the Trouble I've Seen: The Prints and Paintings
of Lamar Baker, February 4- April 14, 1996.* Columbus, Ga.:
The Columbus Museum, 1996.

Phagan, Patricia, ed. *The American Scene and the South: Paintings and Works on Paper, 1930-1946.* Athens: Georgia Museum of Art, 1996.

"Village Iconoclast: A Portfolio of Lithographs by Lamar Baker." *Coronet* 6, no. 3 (July 1939): 92-97.

Zigrosser, Carl. *Lamar Baker: Artist, Draftsman, Etcher, Lithographer.* [New York: Art Students League, n.d.]

GEORGE BELLOWS, 1882-1925

George Bellows attended Ohio State University in his native Columbus, leaving for New York at the beginning of his senior year to enroll in the New York School of Art, run by William Merritt Chase. There he studied briefly under Robert Henri and John Sloan. Although he is best known for his paintings, Bellows installed a lithography press in his studio in 1916 and his contributions in that medium are largely responsible for the growth of lithography as a fine art in America. He worked closely with George Miller, foreman of the stone proofing department of the American Lithographic Company, beginning a long tradition of Miller working directly with artists.

Bellows, George. *George Bellows: Paintings, Drawings, Lithographs: March 15, 1966, through May 1, 1966.* New York: The Gallery of Modern Art including the Huntington Hartford Collection, 1966.

Doezema, Marianne. "The New York City of George Bellows." *Antiques* 141 (March 1992): 480-89.

———. *George Bellows and Urban America.* New Haven: Yale University Press, 1991.

Mason, Lauris. *The Lithographs of George Bellows: A Catalogue Raisonné.* Millwood, N.Y.: KTO Press, 1977.

Myers, Jane, and Linda Ayres. *George Bellows: The Artist and His Lithographs, 1916-1924.* Fort Worth, Tex.: Amon Carter Museum, 1988.

THOMAS HART BENTON, 1889-1975

Born in Neosho, Missouri, Benton trained at the Art Institute of Chicago and the Académie Julien in Paris. He made his first lithograph in 1929, collaborating with master printer George Miller. Throughout the 1920s, the American landscape and the spirit of its people increasingly influenced his work, and by the 1930s he associated with a group of painters known as the Regionalists that included Grant Wood and John Steuart Curry. The Associated American Artists (AAA) distributed many of Benton's lithographs, including *Goin' Home*, as merchandise in department stores and through mail order, democratizing art by making it available to people who lacked the means to buy more costly art.

Adams, Henry. *Thomas Hart Benton: An American Original.* New York: Alfred A. Knopf, 1989.

Fath, Creekmore, ed. *The Lithographs of Thomas Hart Benton.* Austin: University of Texas Press, 1969.

ISABEL BISHOP, 1902-1988

Born in Cincinnati, Ohio, Isabel Bishop grew up in Detroit but went to New York at the age of eighteen to enroll in the School of Applied Design for Women. There she took classes in the Art Students League and became closely linked with instructor Kenneth Hayes Miller and fellow student Reginald Marsh in what has been called the Fourteenth Street School, known for its realistic depiction of the neighborhood around Union Square. Bishop continued to document the Union Square neighborhood through her art into the 1970s.

Newsom, Patricia Paull. "Isabel Bishop." *American Artist* (September 1985):42-45, 90.

Teller, Susan, ed. *Isabel Bishop: Etchings and Aquatints, a Catalogue Raisonné.* New York: Associated American Artists, 1981.

Yglesias, Helen. *Isabel Bishop.* New York: Rizzoli, 1989.

LUCIENNE BLOCH, 1909-1999

Leaving her native Switzerland in 1917, Bloch studied at the Cleveland School of Art. She became a muralist, working for the WPA from 1935 to 1939, and photographer, recording strikes in Flint, Michigan, for *Life* magazine.

"Lucienne Bloch" (obituary). *New York Times*, March 28, 1999.

Figure 31
NICOLAI CIKOVSKY. *On the East River.*
Lithograph. Ca. 1934.
Reproduction courtesy of Nicolai Cikovsky, Jr.

Nicolai Cikovsky emigrated to the United States from the Soviet Union in 1923, a mature artist with years of training behind him. In 1929, he became friends with Raphael Soyer, who had left Russia as a teenager, and shared with him a desire to express through art the experience of the common man. *On the East River* exudes the atmosphere of the piers of New York City during the Depression in a dispassionate manner that offers no illusions.

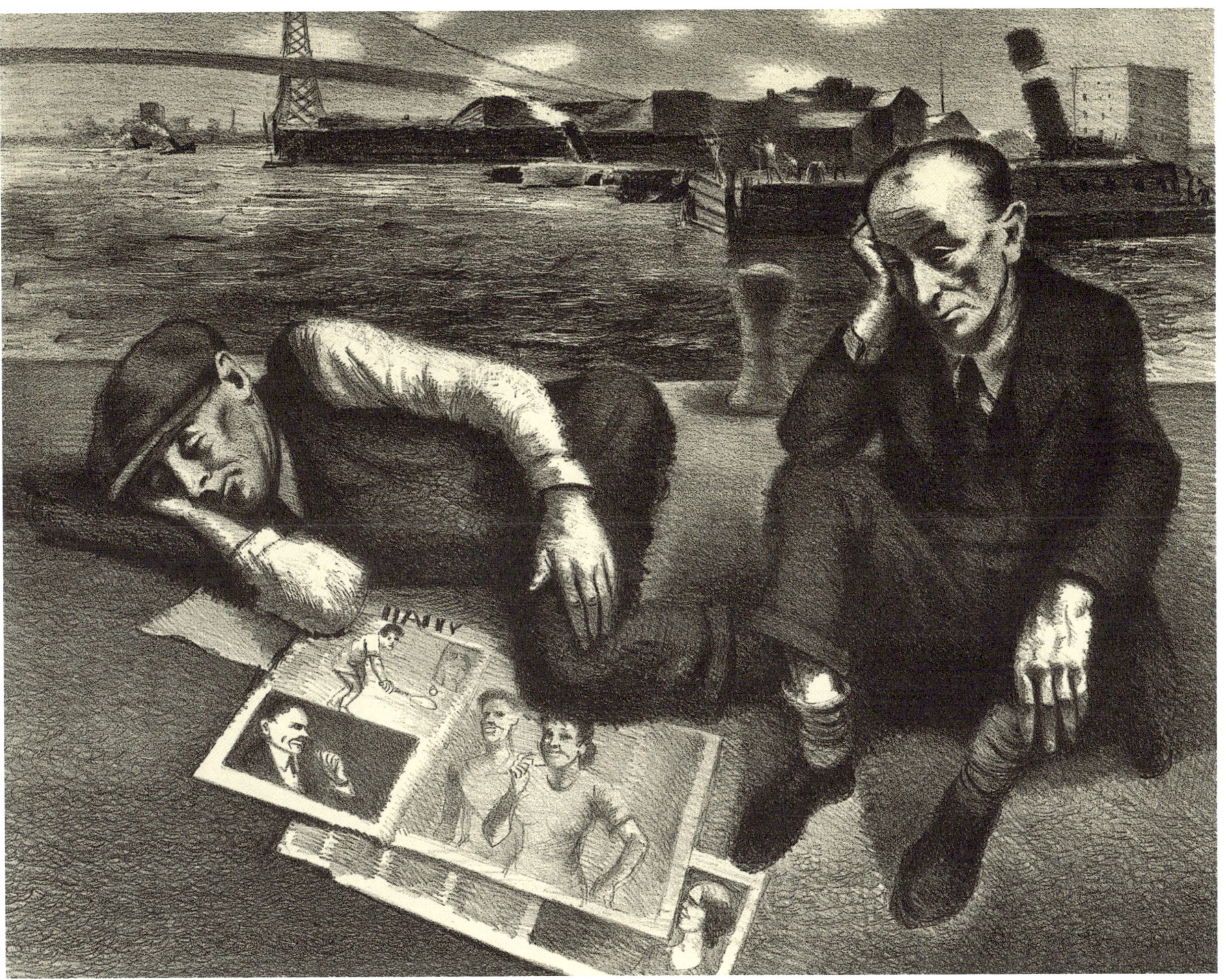

JACOB BURCK, 1907-1982

Jacob Burck was born in Poland and emigrated to the United States at the age of seven. After attending the Cleveland School of Art, he moved to New York to continue his studies at the Art Students League. Briefly in the 1930s, Burck lived in the Soviet Union, working as a mural artist, and returned to the United States to draw cartoons for the Communist Party newspaper, *The Daily Worker*. In 1937 he moved to St. Louis, where for a year he was editorial cartoonist for the *St. Louis Post-Dispatch* along with Daniel Fitzpatrick. Burke then found the job at the *Chicago Times* that he continued for forty-four years, winning the Pulitzer Prize in 1940. In 1953, the U.S. Immigration Service initiated deportation hearings against him, alleging that he belonged to the Communist Party. Burck steadfastly denied membership, arguing that he worked for *The Daily Worker* as a free-lance cartoonist, and the charges were later dropped.

Green, Lloyd. "Prize-Winning Artist. . . ." *Chicago Sun-Times*, May 12, 1982.

"Jacob Burck, Artist" (obituary). *Chicago Sun-Times*, May 15, 1982.

Marshall, Richard. "Burck, Jacob (1904-)." In *The World Encyclopedia of Cartoons*, edited by Maurice Horn, p. 148. Detroit: Gale Research Company, 1980.

NICOLAI CIKOVSKY, 1894-1984

Born in Pinsk, Russia, in 1894, Cikovsky studied at Vilna Art (1910-14), Penza Royal Art School (1914-18), and the Moscow Technical Art Institute (1921-23). He left the newly formed Union of Soviet Socialist Republics during the period of internal struggle that followed the Russian Revolution and immediately began to rebuild his artistic career upon his arrival in New York in 1923, finding his sources of inspiration in the urban environment that greeted him there.

Nicolai Cikovsky. New York: ACA Gallery, [n.d.]

Harrison, Helen A. *Nicolai Cikovsky*. Southampton, N.Y.: Parrish Art Museum, 1980.

GLENN O. COLEMAN, 1887-1932

Born in Ohio, Glenn O. Coleman worked as an apprentice newspaper illustrator before moving to New York City in 1905 to study painting with Robert Henri and Everett Shinn. A classmate of George Bellows, he immediately became associated with liberal movements in art, assisted in organizing the first Independent Exhibition in 1910, and exhibited his work in the Armory Show in 1913. A contributor to *The Masses* before World War I, he was befriended by John Sloan, then a member of the editorial board. Like Sloan, Coleman sketched the world around him and produced many lithographs from his drawings.

Ekedal, Ellen, and Susan Barnes Robinson. *The Spirit of the City: American Urban Paintings, Prints, and Drawings, 1900-1952*. Los Angeles: Loyola Marymount University, 1986.

Glassgold, C. Adolph. *Glenn O. Coleman*. New York: Whitney Museum of American Art, 1932.

More, Hermon. *Glenn O. Coleman Memorial Exhibition, October 18th to November 16, 1932*. New York: Whitney Museum of American Art, 1932.

"Undercurrents of New York Life Sympathetically Depicted in the Drawings of Glenn O. Coleman." *The Craftsman* 17, no. 2 (November 1909):142-49.

JOHN STEUART CURRY, 1897-1946

John Steuart Curry, born in Kansas, studied art at the Kansas City Art Institute and the Art Institute of Chicago before heading east to work as a professional illustrator. His focus on farm subjects and the American Midwest led some to consider him a Regionalist along with Thomas Hart Benton and Grant Wood. Curry himself insisted that subject matter took precedence over style, and he resisted the increasing popularity of modernism in favor of social realism.

Cole, Sylvan, Jr., ed. *The Lithographs of John Steuart Curry: A Catalogue Raisonné*. New York: Associated American Artists, 1976.

Junker, Patricia. *John Steuart Curry: Inventing the Middle West*. New York: Hudson Hills Press, 1998.

Kendall, M. Sue. *Rethinking Regionalism: John Steuart Curry and the Kansas Mural Controversy*. Washington: Smithsonian Institution Press, 1986.

STUART DAVIS, 1892-1964

Born in Philadelphia, Stuart Davis left high school to study painting under Robert Henri, and like his mentor he used the streets as a firsthand source of inspiration during the early years of his career. He portrayed working-class Hoboken, New Jersey, where in 1912 and 1913 he shared a studio with Henry Glintenkamp in the Terminal Building on Hudson Street. Befriending a group of artists, including John Sloan, George Luks, William Glackens, and Everett Shinn, who worked for his father, art editor of the *Philadelphia Press*, he later took part in the exhibition of The Eight in New York.

Hills, Patricia. *Stuart Davis*. New York: Harry N. Abrams, Inc., 1996.

Kelder, Diane, ed. *Stuart Davis*. New York: Praeger Publishers, 1971.

Lane, John R. *Stuart Davis: Art and Art Theory*. New York: The Brooklyn Museum, 1978.

Myers, Jane, ed. *Stuart Davis: Graphic Work and Related Paintings with a Catalogue Raisonné of the Prints*. Fort Worth, Tex: Amon Carter Museum, 1986.

Zurier, Rebecca. *Art for the Masses: A Radical Magazine and Its Graphics, 1911-1917*. Philadelphia: Temple University Press, 1988.

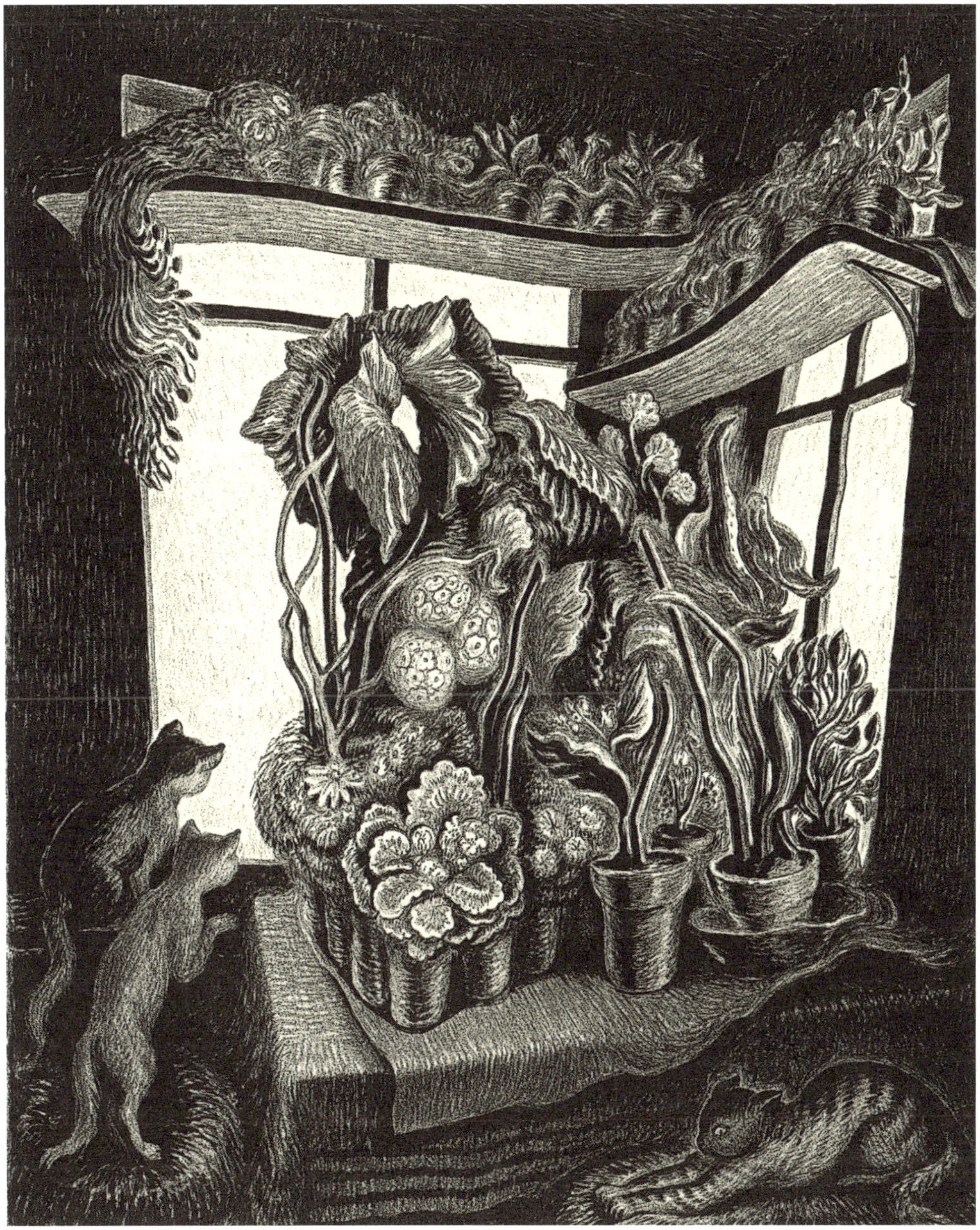

Figure 32
WANDA GÁG. *Winter Garden*.
Lithograph. 1935.
Reproduction courtesy of
the Estate of Wanda Gág.

Wanda Gág, who was a painter, a print-maker, and an award-winning children's book illustrator, said of her work, "A still life is never *still* for me, it is solidified energy." In *Winter Garden* the movement of the cats interacts with the rugs under the plants, which themselves seem to dance.

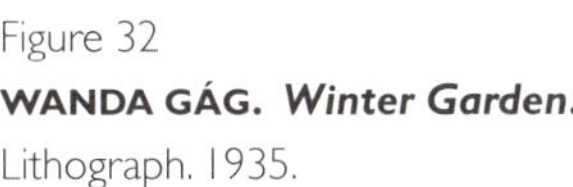

ADOLF DEHN, 1895-1968

Adolf Dehn was born in Minnesota and attended the Minneapolis School of Art in 1914 with the intention of working as a cartoonist and illustrator and seeking to emulate the work of Thomas Nast and Winslow Homer. After graduating in 1917, Dehn set off for New York with a one-year scholarship along with fellow students Wanda Gág and Harry Gottlieb. He studied at the Art Students League with Kenneth Hayes Miller and Boardman Robinson. Robinson encouraged Dehn to move away from cartooning and toward lithography. In 1921, Dehn traveled to Europe, finding employment in Vienna and in Berlin, where he became friends with fellow artist George Grosz, who also influenced Dehn's style. Dehn worked almost exclusively as a draftsman and lithographer until the late 1930s, when he expanded his artistic repertoire to include painting. In 1934, in an attempt to earn money during the Depression, he established the Adolf Dehn Print Club, a mail order project for which *Central Park at Night* was a selection.

Lumsdaine, Joycelyn Pang, and Thomas O'Sullivan, eds. *The Prints of Adolf Dehn: A Catalogue Raisonné*. St. Paul: Minnesota Historical Society Press, 1987.

Pohl, Frances K. *In the Eye of the Storm: An Art of Conscience, 1930-1970*. San Francisco: Pomegranate Artbooks, 1995.

Zigrosser, Carl. *The Artist in America: Twenty-Four Close-Ups of Contemporary Printmakers*, pp. 14-23. New York: Alfred A. Knopf, 1942.

Zurier, Rebecca. *Art for the Masses: A Radical Magazine and Its Graphics, 1911-1917*. Philadelphia: Temple University Press, 1988.

MABEL DWIGHT, 1876-1955

Born in Cincinnati, Mabel Dwight trained as an artist in San Francisco and Paris and, after years of successful work as an illustrator in New York, began making lithographs in 1927, at the age of fifty-two. In 1933 she participated with the Contemporary Print Group and George Miller in creating two influential portfolios of realist prints and from 1935 to 1939 worked for the Federal Art Project of the WPA. A prolific artist, she produced 111 lithographs between 1927 and 1945.

Ekedal, Ellen, and Susan Barnes Robinson. *The Spirit of the City: American Urban Paintings, Prints, and Drawings, 1900-1952*. Los Angeles: Loyola Marymount University, 1986.

Henkes, Robert. *American Women Painters of the 1930s and 1940s: The Lives and Work of Ten Artists*. Jefferson, N.C.: McFarland & Company, Inc., 1991.

Robinson, Susan Barnes, and John Pirog. *Mabel Dwight: A Catalogue Raisonné of the Lithographs*. Washington: Smithsonian Institution Press, 1997.

Zigrosser, Carl. *The Artist in America: Twenty-Four Close-Ups of Contemporary Printmakers*, pp. 145-51. New York: Alfred A. Knopf, 1942.

FRED ELLIS, 1885-1965

After completing an eighth-grade education in his birthplace, Chicago, Fred Ellis began his career as an office boy for the architect Frank Lloyd Wright. He then found work in an engraving shop, had a few months of formal art school training, and took a job as a sign painter for the General Outdoor Advertising Company. In 1919, while working on a scaffold six stories high, Ellis fell to the ground, fracturing thirty-two bones. During the following two years of hospitalization, he began contributing cartoons to the *New Majority*, the newspaper of the Chicago Federation of Labor. Already active in the Industrial Workers of the World (IWW), known as the Wobblies, Ellis met cartoonist Robert Minor, who introduced him to the profession of cartooning. In 1922 he joined the Communist Party. Thanks to Minor, Ellis landed a position as cartoonist for the *Daily Worker*, which moved from Chicago to New York in 1927. In the 1930s, Ellis spent six years in Europe, working in Berlin and Moscow and drawing cartoons for such Russian newspapers as *Trud*, *Izvestia*, and the *Moscow Daily News*. In 1936, he returned to New York to continue his post at the *Daily Worker*, also teaching at the American Artists School.

"The Cover: Fred Ellis." *Courier* 30 (1968).

Durus, Alfred. "Fred Ellis: Artist of the Proletariat." *International Literature* 11 (1935).

Ellis, Robert. Communication with Sara Duke, New York, October 25, 1998.

Garland, Sender (former reporter, *Daily Worker*). Conversation with Sara Duke, October 22, 1998.

Gottfried, Erika (Curator of Nonprint Materials, Robert F. Wagner Labor Archives/Tamiment Library, New York University). Communication with Sara Duke, October 30, 1998.

"Mayfield Library Given Ellis Works." *Post-Standard* (Syracuse, N.Y.), May 19, 1967.

North, Joseph. *Robert Minor: Artist and Crusader*. New York: International Publishers, 1956.

Sullivan, Edmund (Curator, Museum of American Political Life, University of Hartford). Communication with Sara Duke, October 22, 1998.

Zurier, Rebecca (Professor, University of Michigan). Communication with Sara Duke, October 16, 1998.

WANDA GÁG, 1893-1946

A native of New Ulm, Minnesota, Gág received her training first at the Minneapolis School of Art, whose students included Adolf Dehn, Harry Gottlieb, and Elizabeth Olds. A close friend of Dehn's, she moved to New York with him in 1917, having won a scholarship to the Art Students League, where she studied under John Sloan. She attended classes while supporting her family through commercial illustration and writing. Best known as an illustrator of children's books, including the popular *Millions of Cats* (1928) for which she won a Newberry Award, she created paintings, prints, and drawings.

Muessig, Laura (Acting Assistant Registrar, Weisman Art Museum, University of Minnesota, Minneapolis). Communication with Sara Duke, October 2, 1998.

Two Women Printmakers: Wanda Gág and Victoria Huntley. Bethlehem, Conn.: June 1 Gallery, 1986.

The Unseen Wanda Gág: October 26, 1997-January 25, 1998. Minneapolis, Minn.: Frederick R. Weisman Art Museum, 1997.

Winnan, Audur H. *Wanda Gag: A Catalogue Raisonné of the Prints.* Washington: Smithsonian Institution Press, 1993.

Zigrosser, Carl. *The Artist in America: Twenty-Four Close-Ups of Contemporary Printmakers*, pp. 33-44. New York: Alfred A. Knopf, 1942.

HUGO GELLERT, 1892-1985

Born in Budapest, Hungary, in 1892, Hugo Gellert left his native country when he reached draft age to move to New York with his family in 1907. There he took a position in a lithography shop on Horatio Street in the midst of the immigrant community on the Lower East Side, where he made posters for the early movie industry. In 1909 he entered the National Academy of Design, winning cash awards that permitted him to return to Europe in 1914. Angered during World War I by the loss of cousins at the front and the death of a brother who was imprisoned as a conscientious objector, Gellert became increasingly politicized and joined the Communist Party. He returned to the United States and worked for a commercial lithographer while submitting illustrations to the socialist periodical *The Masses*. In the 1920s and 1930s he worked as a staff artist for *Pearson's Magazine*, contributed portraits to *The New Yorker*, designed and painted murals, and published two portfolios of satirical lithographs, *Comrade Gulliver* and *Aesop Said So*, that commented on American life and politics during the Depression. During World War II, Gellert served as chairman of Artists for Victory and from the 1950s through the 1970s used his art to argue for civil rights and promote the activities of labor unions and the Communist Party.

Kisseloff, Jeff. *Hugo Gellert.* New York: Mary Ryan Gallery, 1986.

HENRY GLINTENKAMP, 1887-1946

Born in Augusta, New Jersey, Henry Glintenkamp resided for most of his life in New York City. Between 1903 and 1906 he received formal art instruction at the National Academy of Design and then studied painting with Robert Henri at the New York School of Art, where he met and shared a studio with Glenn O. Coleman and Stuart Davis. He also shared with them an artistic affinity for exploring the more shabby, squalid side of life in New York and New Jersey. His works were exhibited with the Independents in 1910 and in the Armory Show of 1913. Also in 1913, he joined the influential leftist magazine *The Masses* and remained a regular contributor until the magazine's artists' strike of 1916, after which he contributed only intermittently. In 1917 he traveled to Mexico and spent at least seven years there. During the 1930s he traveled briefly in Europe, producing a semi-autobiographical series of woodcuts based on his experiences, attended the American Artists' Congress in 1936, and worked for the WPA.

Glintenkamp, Hendrik. Papers, 1911-60. Microfilm Reel N500. Archives of American Art, Washington, D.C.

Henry Glintenkamp (1887-1946): Ash Can Years to Expressionism, Paintings and Drawings, 1908-1939. New York: Graham, 1981.

Kempe, Richard. *Hendrik Glintenkamp (1887-1987): Un dibujante norteamericano en México, 1917-1920.* México: Museum Estudio Diego Rivera, 1987.

Zurier, Rebecca. *Art for the Masses: A Radical Magazine and Its Graphics, 1911-1917.* Philadelphia: Temple University Press, 1988.

HARRY GOTTLIEB, 1895-1992

Born in Bucharest, Romania, Gottlieb emigrated to Minnesota in 1907 via Ireland. Despite his family's poverty, Gottlieb completed high school in Minneapolis and went on to attend the Minneapolis Institute of Art, with fellow students Adolph Dehn and Wanda Gág. Enlisting in the U.S. Navy during World War I, he served as a military illustrator in New London, Connecticut. In

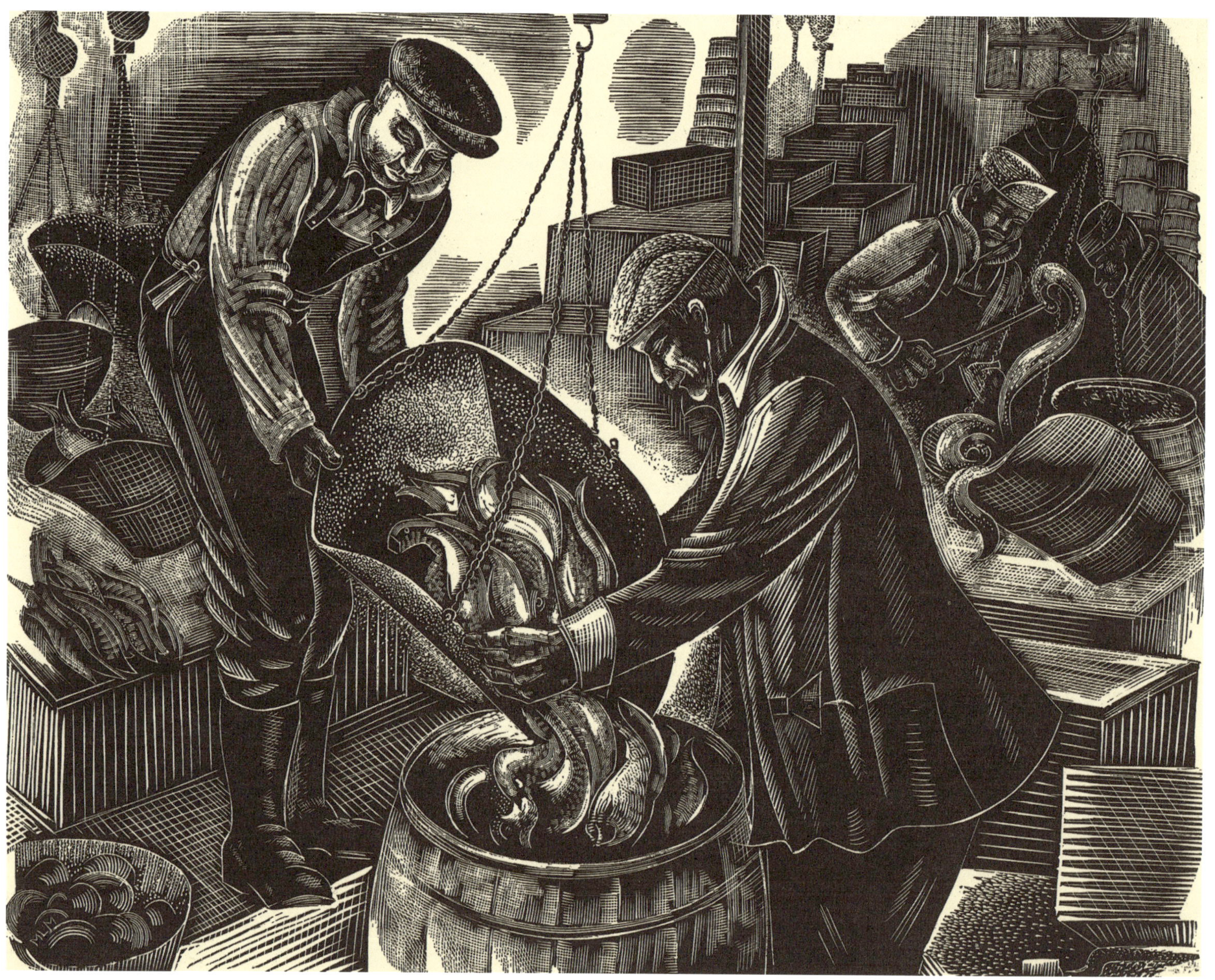

1918, he moved to New York and designed costume and scenery for Eugene O'Neill's plays at the Provincetown Theatre. Five years later he moved to Woodstock, New York, where he spent the next twelve years, with a break for a tour of Europe funded by a Guggenheim Fellowship. Tiring of the provincial life of upstate New York, Gottlieb returned to New York City in 1935. In 1937, as president of the Artists Union, he heard Anthony Velonis propose to the graphics art division of the WPA Federal Art Project that they establish a silkscreen unit. Gottlieb became a founding member of the unit in 1938, along with Louis Lozowick and Elizabeth Olds. Although silkscreen had been used by commercial printers for decades, Velonis, Gottlieb, and Olds understood and exploited its potential as a fine arts process.

Figure 33
M. LOIS MURPHY. *Weighing Fish.*
Wood engraving. Ca. 1936-37.

Lois Murphy made the wood engraving *Weighing Fish* while she was affiliated with the WPA Federal Art Project in New York City in 1936-37.

Gottlieb, Harry. Vertical file. National Museum of American Art/National Portrait Gallery Library, Smithsonian Institution, Washington, D.C.

Harry Gottlieb: The Silkscreen and Social Concern in the WPA Era. New Brunswick, N.J.: The Jane Voorhees Zimmerli Art Museum, Rutgers University, 1983.

BLANCHE GRAMBS, born 1916

Born in Beijing, China, to American parents, Blanche Mary Grambs arrived in New York in March 1934 with a full scholarship to attend the Art Students League. It was a politically contentious time, and she joined the Artists' Union in 1935. She studied with Harry Sternberg and took courses in Marxist economics at the New Workers School. In 1936 Grambs joined the Federal Art Project of the Works Progress Administration, earning enough money to maintain her studio on Fourteenth Street, an area where many radicals congregated. She worked as an active printmaker for only six years, from 1934 to 1939. After 1939, Grambs became an illustrator for *Woman's Day* and illustrated various children's books.

Wechsler, James. "The Great Depression and the Prints of Blanche Grambs." *Print Quarterly* 13, no. 4 (1996):376-96.

WILLIAM GROPPER, 1897-1977

William Gropper dropped out of school at age fourteen to help support his family. He worked in New York sweatshops by day while studying under Robert Henri and George Bellows at the Ferrer Center at night, winning a scholarship to the New York School of Fine and Applied Art in 1916. Three years later he began working as an illustrator and cartoonist for the *New York Tribune*, encountering radical ideas while covering an Industrial Workers of the World meeting. He was fired by the *Tribune* in 1921 when his ideas became too leftist for the editorial staff, but he had already begun to contribute to such progressive publications as the *Liberator* and the *Dial*. In 1942 the Metropolitan Museum of Art awarded him first prize in the *Artists for Victory* exhibition and in 1945 he was elected vice president of the association Artists for Victory. Although never a member of the Communist Party, Gropper was blacklisted in 1953 by the House Un-American Activities Committee as a result of his outspokenness on labor issues and occasional professional trips to Russia.

Gropper, William. Correspondence of the Region 2 Office (New York area) with artists, 1933-34. Records of the PWAP, Record Group 121, National Archives. Microfilm Reel DC113. Archives of American Art, Washington, D.C .

Gropper, 1940. New York: ACA Gallery, 1940.

Gropper, 1944. New York: ACA Gallery, 1944.

Hills, Patricia, "The Career and Art of William Gropper—In Brief." In *The Art of William Gropper.* Framingham, Mass.: Danforth Museum, 1983.

Landau, Ellen G. *Artists for Victory: An Exhibition Catalog.* Washington: Library of Congress, 1983.

Lozowick, Louis. *William Gropper.* Philadelphia: Art Alliance Press; New York: Cornwall Books, 1983.

William Gropper Revisited. New York: Sid Deutsch Gallery, 1989.

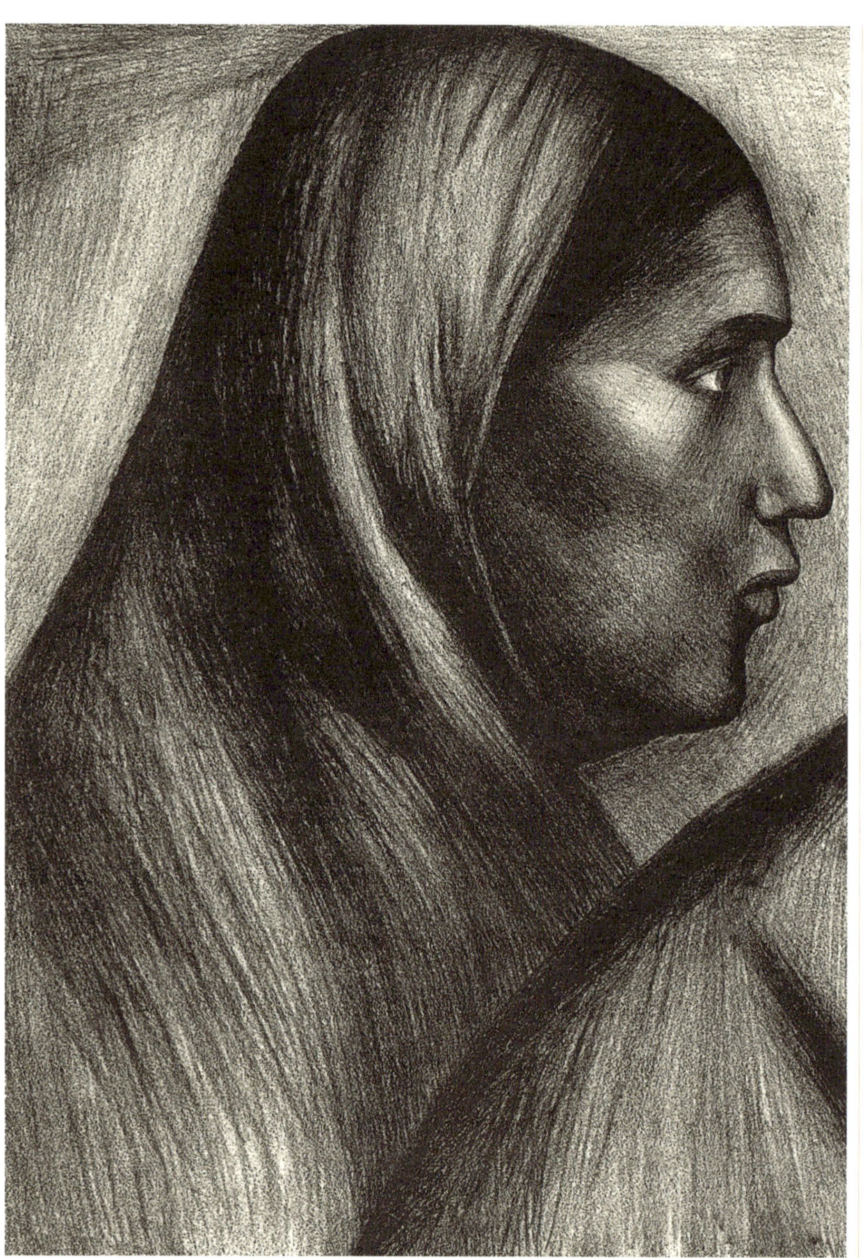

ROBERT GWATHMEY, 1903-1988

Between 1924 and 1930, Robert Gwathmey studied art at the North Carolina State College in Raleigh, the Maryland Institute of Art in Baltimore, and the Pennsylvania Academy of the Fine Arts in Philadelphia. He then taught at Beaver College in Jenkintown, Pennsylvania, between 1931 and 1937, escaping some of the worst consequences of the Depression and enjoying enough free time

Figure 34
JOSÉ CLEMENTE OROZCO.
Mujer mexicana.
Lithograph. 1929.
Copyright © Estate of José Clemente Orozco / SOMAAP, Mexico / Licensed by VAGA, New York, N.Y.
Reproducción autorizada por el Instituto Nacional de Bellas Artes y Literatura.

Mujer mexicana, also called *Cabeza de mujer,* was one of José Clemente Orozco's earliest lithographs, based on the fresco he created for his alma mater, the National Preparatory School in Mexico City. It is taken from the panel called *The Return to Labor.* Using the same geometricized manner typical of pre-Columbian art that he used in the fresco, Orozco nevertheless created a new work which, although a detail, stands as more than a fragment of the larger work from which it was drawn.

to pursue his art and travel to New York. He taught art at the Carnegie Institute in Pittsburgh between 1938 and 1942 before moving to New York to take a teaching position at Cooper Union. While living in Pittsburgh, Gwathmey made his first screenprint, experimenting with the relatively new medium promoted by Anthony Velonis, who proposed the silkscreen unit of the Federal Art Project in 1938. Gwathmey added other printmaking techniques to his oeuvre in the 1960s and continued to paint and make prints into the 1980s.

Lerner, Abram. *Gwathmey: Works from 1941-1983.* East Hampton, N.Y.: Guild Hall Museum, 1984.

Piehl, Charles K. "Robert Gwathmey: The Social and Historical Context of a Southerner's Art in the Mid-Twentieth Century." *Arts in Virginia* 29, no. 1 (1989):2-15.

———. "The Southern Social Art of Robert Gwathmey," *Transactions of the Wisconsin Academy of Sciences, Arts, and Letters* 73 (1985):54-62.

Williams, Reba White, "The Prints of Robert Gwathmey." In *Hot Off the Press: Prints and Politics*, edited by Linda Tyler and Barry Walker, pp. 33-56. Albuquerque, N.M.: Tamarind Institute, 1994.

JOSEPH HIRSCH, 1910-1981

Joseph Hirsch's career as an artist began at age seventeen when he received a four-year scholarship to the Philadelphia College of Art in his native city. He first received notice as a painter and then ventured into lithography in 1938. Hirsch taught at the Art Students League and other institutions and served as an artist and war correspondent for both the U.S. Army and the U.S. Navy during World War II.

Cole, Sylvan, comp. and ed. *The Graphic Work of Joseph Hirsch.* New York: Associated American Artists, 1970.

Hirsch, Joseph. Vertical file. National Museum of American Art/National Portrait Gallery Library, Smithsonian Institution, Washington, D.C.

VICTORIA HUTSON HUNTLEY, 1900-1971

A native of New Jersey, Victoria Hutson studied at the New York School of Fine and Applied Art and the Art Students League before taking a teaching position at the College of Industrial Arts in Denton, Texas, in 1921. When she returned to New York she took classes from Kenneth Hayes Miller and studied mural painting with William C. Palmer. After her first solo exhibition at the Weyhe Gallery in 1930, Huntley turned her attention to lithography. Her interest in industrial America, which dominated her work in the 1930s, gave way to an interest in birds, flowers, and landscapes in the 1940s, but she returned to industrial themes when she moved to Chicago in the 1950s.

Huntley, Victoria Hutson. Correspondence of the Region 2 Office (New York area) with artists, 1933-34. Records of the PWAP, Record Group 121, National Archives. Microfilm Reel DC113. Archives of American Art, Washington, D.C.

———. *Portraits of Plants and Places by Victoria Hutson Huntley, A.N.A.* New York: Print Club, 1946.

"Lithographer." *Washington Star*, November 7, 1954.

Two Women Printmakers: Wanda Gág and Victoria Huntley. Bethlehem, Conn.: June 1 Gallery, 1986.

JOE JONES, 1909-1963

Joe Jones emerged on the art scene in 1931 as a self-taught artist. Born in St. Louis, he quit school at age fifteen to work as a house painter and decorator. Winning his first award in 1931, he gained the attention of wealthy St. Louis patrons and in 1933 traveled to the artists' colony in Provincetown, Massachusetts, with financial backing. He returned with the pronouncement that he had joined the Communist Party. His political activities alienated his patrons, so Jones signed up for the short-lived Public Works of Art Project in 1934. At the same time, he offered free art classes for those artists, mainly African Americans, who could not participate in the federal program. He moved to New York that same year as local pressures mounted against him. Although he painted in both the social realist and Regionalist styles, he felt uncomfortable about his association with the Regionalists, arguing that they were too conservative. His commitment to Communism declined with the Second World War, when he was assigned to the War Art Unit and then did a stint as a war correspondent for *Life*. Jones remained dedicated to portraying the American landscape throughout his career.

Francey, Mary. *Depression Printmakers as Workers: Re-Defining Traditional Interpretations.* Salt Lake City: Utah Museum of Fine Arts, University of Utah, 1988.

Graphic Excursions—American Prints in Black and White, 1900-1950: Selections from the Collection of Reba and Dave Williams. Essays by Karen F. Beall and David W. Kiehl. Boston: D.R. Godine in association with the American Federation of Arts, 1991

Iarocci, Louisa. "The Changing American Landscape: The Art and Politics of Joe Jones." *Gateway Heritage*, Fall 1991: 68-75.

Joe Jones & J. B. Turnbull: Visions of the Midwest in the 1930s. Milwaukee, Wis.: Patrick and Beatrice Haggerty Museum of Art, Marquette University, 1987.

Pohl, Frances K. *In the Eye of the Storm: An Art of Conscience, 1930-1970.* San Francisco: Pomegranate Artbooks, 1995.

SAUL KOVNER, 1904-1981

Born in Russia, Saul Kovner emigrated to New York City with his family about 1912 and began to study art at the Pratt Institute, subsequently studying painting and printmaking with William Auerbach-Levy and drawing with Charles Hawthorne at the National Academy of Design. During the 1920s and 1930s, he maintained a studio near Central Park, taught art classes, and created paintings, prints, and drawings of the city streets and locales and their denizens. Between 1935 and 1940, he participated as a muralist in the Federal Art Project of the WPA. After World War II, he moved to Burbank, California, where he continued to paint and teach.

Kovner, Saul. Microfilm reel 1090. Archives of American Art, Washington, D.C.

Lovoos, Janice. "The Art of Saul Kovner." *American Artist* 32, no. 2 (February 1968): 40-45, 63-65.

North, Bill, and Stephen H. Goddard. *Rural America: Prints from the Collection of Steven Schmidt,* p. 36. Lawrence: Spencer Museum of Art, University of Kansas, 1993.

CLARE LEIGHTON, 1898-1989

Born in London, England, in 1898, Clare Leighton was raised in a home that served as a salon for literati, social reformers, and intellectuals. Although she had already illustrated her father's books, her formal schooling did not begin until 1918 when she entered the Brighton School of Art. Leighton made her first wood engraving in 1923, while enrolled at the London Central School. She also studied at the Slade School of Fine Arts of the University of London. A prolific artist, she created about seven hundred wood engravings during her lifetime, as well as designs for stained glass windows, mosaics, and glassware. In 1939 Leighton settled permanently in the United States, where she became a citizen in 1945. Among the books she illustrated were Thomas Hardy's *Return of the Native* and *Under the Greenwood Tree,* her own book *Sometime, Never,* and a four-volume edition of *The Works of Henry David Thoreau.* Leighton also designed stained glass windows for the Worcester Cathedral in Worcester, Massachusetts.

Clare Leighton, an Exhibition: American Sheaves / English Seed Corn. Boston, Mass.: Boston Public Library, 1977.

Clare Leighton. Chronology supplied by her nephew, David Roland Leighton, December 1998.

Francey, Mary. *Depression Printmakers as Workers: Re-Defining Traditional Interpretations.* Salt Lake City: Utah Museum of Fine Arts, University of Utah, 1988.

Hamilton, James. *Wood Engraving & the Woodcut in Britain, c.1890-1990.* London: Barrie & Jenkins, 1994.

Jaffe, Patricia. *Women Engravers.* Camden Town, London: Virago, 1990.

"Leighton, Clare." Vertical file. National Museum of American Art/National Portrait Gallery Library, Smithsonian Institution, Washington, D.C.

McCurdy, Linda (Director of Research Services, Rare Book, Manuscript, and Special Collections Library, Duke University). Communication with Sara Duke, October 29, 1998.

MICHAEL LENSON, 1903-1971

After emigrating from Galich, Russia, as a child in 1913, Michael Lenson enrolled in the National Academy of Design in New York in 1920. In 1928 he won the prestigious Chaloner Prize for Painting, which permitted him to travel to Europe for four years and study for extensive periods at the Slade School of the University of London and at the Académie des Beaux-Arts in Paris. He returned to the United States in 1933 and received critical success at his one-man exhibition

Figure 35

RAPHAEL SOYER. *Waterfront.*
Lithograph. 1934.
Copyright © Raphael Soyer, reproduced by permission of the Estate of Raphael Soyer, courtesy Forum Gallery, New York.

In the early 1920s, Raphael Soyer applied the early academic training he had received at the National Academy of Design to the life he found in the districts of New York City: "I wandered all over the city, from east to west with sketchbook and pencil. There were not yet the highways along the East and Hudson rivers. It was easy to get to the river's edge and draw, unobserved, people on docks and piers and naked boys diving into the water." Without being sentimental or moralizing, Soyer's *Waterfront* projects empathy for the victims of the Depression.

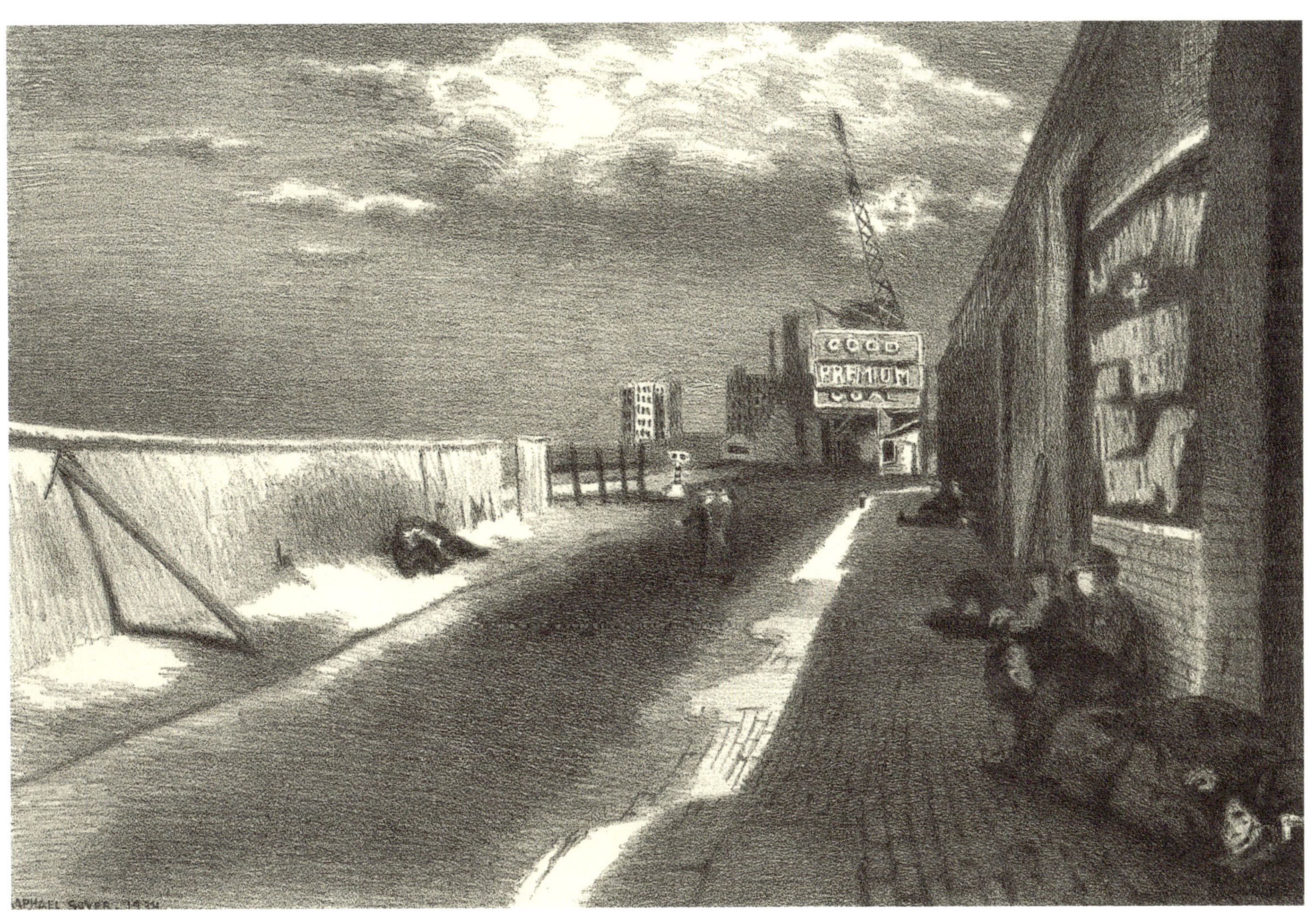
GOOD
PREMIUM
COAL
RAPHAEL SOYER 1934

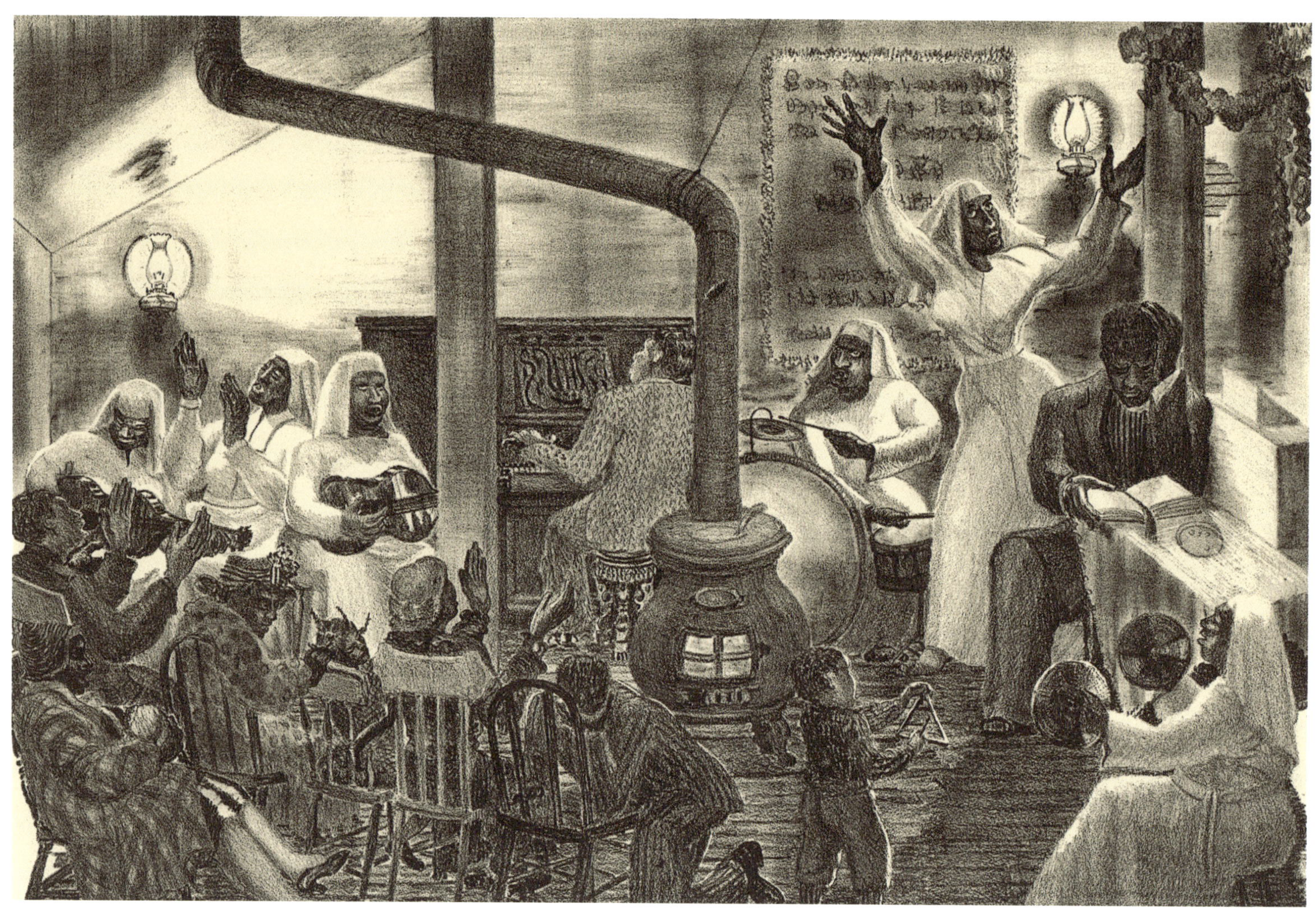

at the Caz-Delbo Gallery. Because it was the height of the Depression, his success did not translate into income, so he made his way to New Jersey, where he created murals for the WPA Federal Art Project.

Lenson, Michael. *Real & Surreal: Paintings from the 30s, 40s & 50s: Michael Lenson, 1903-1971.* New York: Janet Marqusee Fine Arts, 1993.

Figure 36
PRENTISS TAYLOR. *Assembly Church.*
Lithograph. 1936.
Reproduction courtesy of
the Estate of Prentiss Taylor.

Prentiss Taylor began his artistic career working in an abstract style, but adopted realism soon after beginning to study under Charles Locke at the Art Students League in 1931. His interest in African American life and culture deepened during his publishing collaboration with the author and poet Langston Hughes that same year and through his intermittent travels to South Carolina, including a 1934 trip supported by the New York City Public Works of Art Project. Taylor made 137 lithographs in his lifetime, varying in style and theme, his subject matter ranging from life in the American South to the architecture of Spain.

MARTIN LEWIS, 1881-1962

Born in Australia, Martin Lewis left home at the age of fifteen, studied briefly at the Art Society in Sydney, and emigrated to the United States in 1900. He supported himself by doing commercial work, leaving his adopted country for Japan in 1920 but returning to settle permanently in New York in 1922. Although Lewis had made a series of etchings between 1915 and 1920—frequently working directly on copper—he did not turn seriously to printmaking until 1925. In 1929, after a critically and financially successful solo exhibition at the Kennedy Gallery, he ceased his commercial work. Although many artists, including Thomas Hart Benton and John Steuart Curry, used prints as a means to rework compositions in paint, Lewis instead created original compositions in his prints. In 1940, Lewis gave 200 impressions of *Boss of the Block* to the Art Students League, where he was an instructor, for the school to use as a means to raise money.

McCarron, Paul. *The Prints of Martin Lewis: A Catalogue Raisonné.* Bronxville, N.Y.: M. Hausberg, 1995.

LOUIS LOZOWICK, 1892-1973

Lozowick was born in Ludvinovka, Russia, and under the guidance of an older brother enrolled in 1903 in the Kiev Art School. In 1906 he followed his brother to New York, where he completed high school. He attended the National Academy of Design from 1912 to 1915, afterward earning a degree from Ohio State University. Between 1920 and 1924, Lozowick lived in Europe, where he was influenced by both the Cubist and Futurist movements. While living in Berlin in 1923, he began to make lithographs. After his return to the United States, he worked for the WPA and became active in the American Artists' Congress. He continued to make prints into the 1970s.

Flint, Janet. *The Prints of Louis Lozowick: A Catalogue Raisonné.* New York: Hudson Hills Press, 1982.

Francey, Mary. *Depression Printmakers as Workers: Re-Defining Traditional Interpretations.* Salt Lake City: Utah Museum of Fine Arts, University of Utah, 1988.

Lozowick, Louis. *Survivor from a Dead Age: The Memoirs of Louis Lozowick.* Edited by Virginia Hagelstein Marquardt. Washington: Smithsonian Institution Press, 1997.

————. Vertical file. National Museum of American Art / National Portrait Gallery Library, Smithsonian Institution, Washington, D.C.

KYRA MARKHAM, 1891-1967

Born Elaine Hyman, Markham quit high school at age sixteen to attend classes at the Art Institute of Chicago, in her native city. At eighteen, she became an actress in Chicago's Little Theater, where she met and became involved with the novelist Theodore Dreiser. Their relationship ended with Markham's move in 1916 to join the Provincetown Players theatrical troupe in Provincetown, Massachusetts, where she supplemented her acting income by painting murals and working as an illustrator. In 1930, Markham returned to the study of art at the Art Students

League in New York, taking up lithography in 1934. Like many other Depression era artists, she found work with the WPA Federal Art Project, enrolling in the program between 1935 and 1937. Markham continued making prints during the next decade, before moving to Vermont, where she and her husband managed a working farm until 1957; she died in Port-au-Prince, Haiti.

Kyra Markham: American Fantasist. New York: The Witkin Gallery, 1981.

Markham, Kyra. American Artists Group Records, 1934-65. Microfilm Reel NAG5 66-106. Archives of American Art, Washington, D.C.

————. Vertical file. National Museum of American Art/National Portrait Gallery Library, Smithsonian Institution, Washington, D.C.

Pohl, Frances K. *In the Eye of the Storm: An Art of Conscience, 1930-1970.* San Francisco: Pomegranate Artbooks, 1995.

Popper, Merna. *Kyra Markham: Graphic Works, 1934-1935.* New York: Sarah Lawrence College, 1977.

ROBERT MINOR, 1884-1952

Robert Minor began his career as a cartoonist in 1904 at the *San Antonio Gazette* and the following year went to the *St. Louis Post-Dispatch*, where he was exposed to the radical ideas that marked the rest of his life. Already one of the foremost editorial cartoonists in America when he moved to New York to take a position at the *New York World* in 1912, he began also to do work for the socialist periodical *The Masses*, becoming a major contributor after 1915. When, like many leftist cartoonists, he refused to support America's war effort during World War I, he lost his position in the mainstream press. He contributed cartoons to the *Daily Worker* and traveled through Europe, ultimately giving up drawing altogether to become a political activist in the Communist Party in 1926.

North, Joseph. *Robert Minor: Artist and Crusader.* New York: International Publishers, 1956.

Zurier, Rebecca. *Art for the Masses: A Radical Magazine and Its Graphics, 1911-1917.* Philadelphia: Temple University Press, 1988.

M. LOIS MURPHY, 1901-1962

Minnie Lois Murphy was born in Lyons, Kansas. She attended the University of California at Los Angeles and Columbia University before studying with Boardman Robinson and George Grosz at the Art Students League in New York.

The Federal Art Project: American Prints from the 1930s in the Collection of the University of Michigan Museum of Art. Ann Arbor, Mich.: The Museum, 1985.

Murphy, M. Lois. Vertical file. National Museum of American Art/National Portrait Gallery Library, Smithsonian Institution, Washington, D.C.

Seaton, Elizabeth G. (Ph.D. candidate, Northwestern University). Communication with Sara Duke, October 17, 1998.

PABLO O'HIGGINS, 1904-1983

Born Paul Higgins in Salt Lake City, Utah, the young artist first studied at the School of Fine Arts in San Diego. His admiration for the Mexican muralists led O'Higgins south to Mexico City, where he became an apprentice to Diego Rivera from 1924 to 1928. Driven by Marxist theory to act politically, he formed La Liga de Escritores y Artistas Revolucionarios (LEAR) in 1933. In 1937, Pablo O'Higgins became a founding member of the print workshop Taller de Gráfica Popular. Best remembered as a muralist, he also created paintings and made prints.

Oles, James. *South of the Border: Mexico in the American Imagination, 1917-1947.* Trans. Marta Ferragut. Washington: Smithsonian Institution Press, 1993.

Poniatowska, Elena, and Gilberto Bosques. *Pablo O'Higgins.* Mexico: Fondo Editorial de la Plástica Mexicana, fideicomiso en el Banco Nacional de Comercio Exterior, 1984.

ELIZABETH OLDS, 1896-1991

Elizabeth Olds trained at the University of Minnesota, the Minneapolis School of Art, and the Art Students League under George Luks, an Ashcan School printmaker, eventually becoming his assistant. She was the first woman artist to receive a Guggenheim Fellowship, which allowed her to study art in Europe in 1926-27. Upon her return to the United States, she received a commission that took her to Omaha, Nebraska, where in 1932 she learned the process of lithography, from grinding the stones to cranking the printing press. She worked for the Omaha Public Works of Art Project. In the fall of 1935, Olds joined the New York City WPA Federal Art Project. She began experimenting with the screenprint process under Anthony Velonis in 1938, as one of the founding members of the

WPA Federal Art Project silkscreen unit. In the
1930s and 1940s she created images in the social
realist mode to express solidarity with struggling
workers, summing up her own work and that of a
generation of artists: "American artists have lately
chosen to portray our own life. We find our subject on the streets, in the factory, the machines
and workers of industry and on the farm. We aim
to picture truly the life about us as the people we
are in reference to the forces that make us. We
choose all sides of life, searching for the vital and
significant."

Olds, Elizabeth. Papers, 1917-76. Microfilm Reel 2976.
Archives of American Art, Washington, D.C.

Figure 37
ELIZABETH WHITE.
All God's Chillun' Got Wings!
Soft-ground etching and aquatint. Ca. 1933.
Reproduction courtesy of the Sumter
Gallery of Art, Sumter, South Carolina.

Born in South Carolina, Elizabeth White
went north to Philadelphia—and later to
the MacDowell Colony in Peterborough,
New Hampshire—for formal art study. For
most of her life she lived in the South, and
the landscape and people of her native
region remained a dominant and evocative
presence in her work.

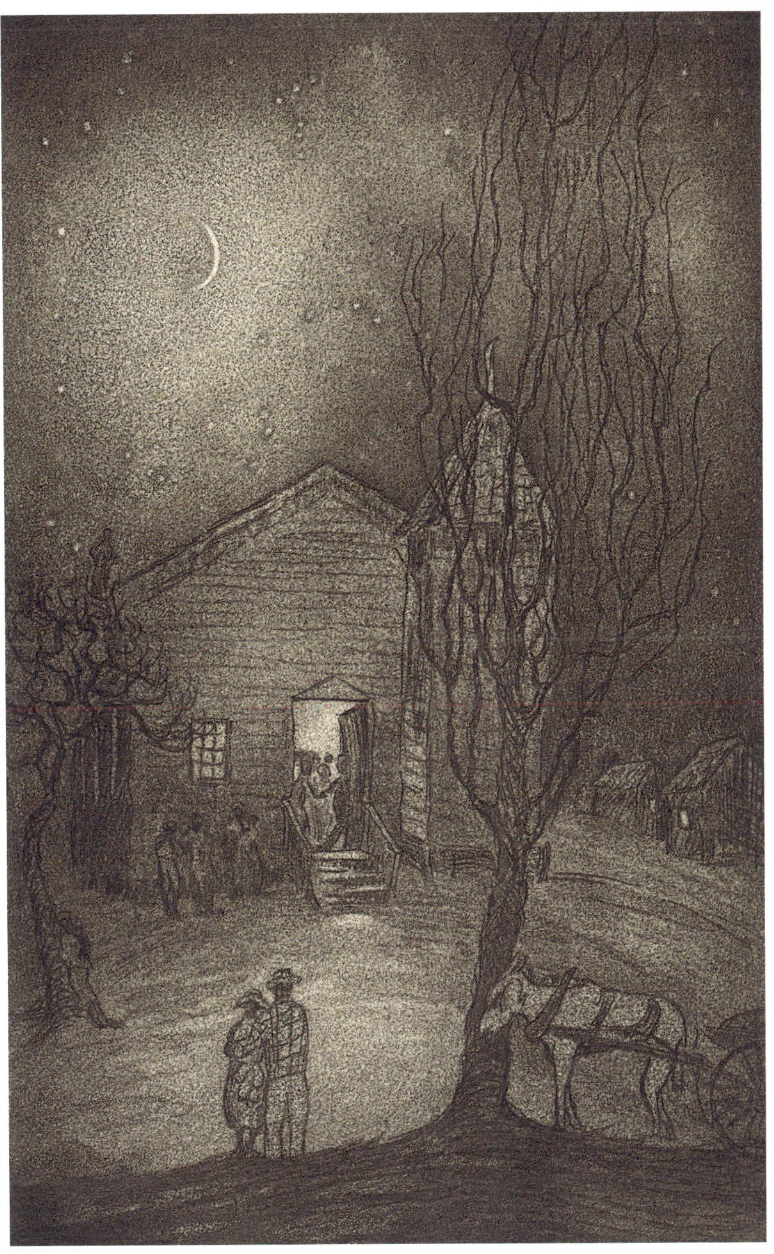

————. Vertical file. National Museum of American Art/National Portrait Gallery Library, Smithsonian Institution, Washington, D.C.

Pohl, Frances K. *In the Eye of the Storm: An Art of Conscience, 1930-1970.* San Francisco: Pomegranate Artbooks, 1995.

Prescott, Kenneth W., and Susan E. Arthur. *Elizabeth Olds Retrospective Exhibition: Paintings, Drawings, Prints.* Austin, Tex.: The RGK Foundation, 1986.

JOSÉ CLEMENTE OROZCO, 1883-1949

Born in the state of Jalisco, Orozco moved to Mexico City as a child, studying agriculture before attending the National University of Mexico to specialize in mathematics and architectural drawing. Best known as a mural painter, he produced prints to secure a wider audience for his art. Orozco's interest in graphic arts came as a natural part of his training under José Guadalupe Posada, the provocative and prolific printmaker whose influence extended far beyond his native Mexico. As a result of his frequent trips to the United States and the murals he created in California, in New York City, and at Dartmouth College in Hanover, New Hampshire, Orozco in turn encouraged many American artists.

The Graphic Works of Orozco. Washington: Pan American Union, 1952.

Helm, MacKinley. *Man of Fire: J. C. Orozco, an Interpretative Memoir.* Westport, Conn.: Greenwood Press, 1971.

Hopkins, Jon H. *Orozco: A Catalogue of His Graphic Work.* Flagstaff: Northern Arizona University Publications, 1967.

Orozco, Clemente. "José Clemente Orozco: Catalogo razonado." [Mexico], copyright 1997. Bound manuscript. Prints and Photographs Division, Library of Congress.

Orozco, January 5-31, 1965. San Diego: Fine Arts Gallery of San Diego, 1965.

JAMES PENNEY, 1910-1982

At the height of the Depression, James Penney, a native of Missouri, received a degree from the University of Kansas, where he had studied painting, and was granted a scholarship to attend the Art Students League in New York. Enrolled there between 1931 and 1934, he studied lithography with Charles Locke and painting with George Grosz. Penney found his primary source of income in New York to be the WPA Federal Art Project, where in 1935 he began working as a muralist. He secured a faculty position at Hunter College in 1941, briefly taught at Bennington College in Vermont, and in 1948 began a twenty-one-year tenure as a studio art professor at Hamilton College in upstate New York.

James Penney: A Retrospective Exhibition of Paintings, 1933-1977. Utica, N.Y.: Museum of Art, Munson-Williams-Proctor Institute, 1977.

James Penney, 1910-1982: A Memorial Exhibition November 19-December 23, 1983. Clinton, N.Y.: The Fred L. Emerson Gallery, Hamilton College, 1983.

ALBERT POTTER, 1903-1937

Born in Russia, Albert Potter emigrated to the United States as an infant and grew up in Providence, Rhode Island. He attended the Rhode Island School of Design, winning the Trustee's Postgraduate Scholarship in 1927, which permitted him to study under English printmaker Frank Brangwyn. In 1928, Potter returned to the United States and lived in New York. He briefly attended the New York Industrial School before participating in a federal art project at Welfare Island in 1934. By 1936, he had returned to Rhode Island and signed on with the Rhode Island WPA Federal Art Project. The artist's work spans less than a decade, however, because Potter's life was cut short in 1937 when he fell off a cliff while sketching in Rhode Island.

Albert Potter: Brother, Can You Spare a Dime? New York: Susan Teller Gallery, 1991.

ANTON REFREGIER, 1905-1979

Born in 1905 in Moscow, Refregier left Russia for Paris at the age of fifteen and there became an apprentice to the sculptor Vassilief. At the invitation of an uncle, he emigrated to the United States in the early 1920s, later receiving a scholarship to attend the Rhode Island School of Design. In 1928, after completing his studies, he went to New York with the hope of becoming a mural painter but found himself working instead for interior decorators. The politicized atmosphere of the art scene in the city led him to work for trade union journals. He became active in the John Reed Club, the American Artists' Congress, and the Artists Union. Under the WPA Federal Art Project, Refregier finally achieved his goal of becoming a mural painter, extending art to all sorts of public buildings through murals he completed in supermarkets, restaurants, and a housing development. Refregier also designed store windows, tableware, and fabrics.

"Anton Refregier, Murals Painter" (obituary). *New York Times*, October 13, 1979.

Park, Marlene, and Gerald E. Markowitz. *Democratic Vistas: Post Offices and Public Art in the New Deal.* Philadelphia: Temple University Press, 1984.

Pohl, Frances K. *In the Eye of the Storm: An Art of Conscience, 1930-1970.* San Francisco: Pomegranate Artbooks, 1995.

Refregier, Anton. Oral history interview conducted by Joseph Trovator for the New Deal and the Arts Oral History Project, Archives of American Art, Washington, D.C.

—————. Vertical file. National Museum of American Art/National Portrait Gallery Library, Smithsonian Institution, Washington, D.C.

DIEGO RIVERA, 1886-1957

Diego Rivera was born in Guanjuato, Mexico, grew up in Mexico City, and attended the San Carlos Academy of Fine Arts. He also studied in the studio of one of the finest graphic artists of the day, José Guadalupe Posada. Between 1907 and 1921, Rivera traveled in Europe, experimenting with a number of artistic styles, cubism in particular. Upon his return to Mexico, Rivera and his fellow artists José Orozco and David Siqueiros initiated the Mexican mural renaissance. With a commission from the U.S. ambassador to Mexico, Dwight W. Morrow, Rivera painted a mural for the loggia of the Palacio de Cortés in Cuernavaca. After completing the mural, between December 1929 and November 1930, Rivera embarked on a lengthy residence in the United States. During this period he exerted a profound influence on American artists through retrospective exhibitions held at the California Palace of the Legion of Honor in San Francisco and the Museum of Modern Art in New York City and through numerous notable and controversial murals painted in those cities and at the Institute of Arts in Detroit, Michigan.

Diego Rivera: Selected Works, 1918-1949. San Francisco: The Mexican Museum, 1985.

Wolfe, Bertram D. *The Fabulous Life of Diego Rivera.* Chelsea, Mich.: Scarborough House, 1990.

JAMES N. ROSENBERG, 1874-1970

Born in Pittsburgh, Pennsylvania, James Rosenberg grew up in New York City, attending Columbia University and graduating from Columbia Law School in 1898. Even after becoming a successful bankruptcy lawyer in Manhattan, Rosenberg nevertheless continued to cultivate a passion for art, which led to his becoming a collector. He "loved the adventure of self-expression," and thus painted and made prints in his spare time, discovering lithography under George Miller's tutelage in 1919. In 1922, Rosenberg became joint owner of the New Gallery, selling objects by Modigliani and Matisse that he acquired on travels through Europe. When he retired from his law firm in 1942, he continued to paint and to promote the arts.

Graphic Excursions—American Prints in Black and White, 1900-1950: Selections from the Collection of Reba and Dave Williams. Essays by Karen F. Beall and David W. Kiehl. Boston: D.R. Godine in association with the American Federation of Arts, 1991.

Rosenberg, James N. *Painter's Self-Portrait.* New York: Crown Publishers, Inc., 1958.

GEORGES SCHREIBER, 1904-1977

Georges Schreiber was born in Brussels, Belgium, of German-Jewish parents. The family returned to Germany after World War I. There Schreiber was educated in the French tradition of *peintre-graveur* at the Kunstgewerbeschule in Elberfeld and at the academies of fine arts in Berlin and Dusseldorf. In addition, he made study trips to the museums of London, Florence, Rome, and Paris. He began work as a freelance artist in 1925, when he was hired by the *Koelner Tageblatt*, a daily newspaper published in Cologne. After emigrating to the United States in 1928, Schreiber contributed illustrations to the *New York Times* and the *New York Post.* In 1936 he enrolled in the WPA Federal Art Project and toured all forty-eight states in the next three years, creating representational lithographs around the country.

Georges Schreiber: Paintings and Works on Paper of the 1930s and 1940s. New York: Susan Teller Gallery, 1995.

Georges Schreiber: Symphonic Variations, 1971-73. New York: Kennedy Galleries, 1973.

Georges Schreiber: Watercolors 1969-1970. New York: Kennedy Galleries, 1970.

Lithography by Georges Schreiber: A Retrospective Exhibit. Washington: Klutznick Exhibit Hall, B'nai B'rith Building, 1964.

Schreiber, Georges. Vertical file. National Museum of American Art/National Portrait Gallery Library, Smithsonian Institution, Washington, D.C.

Schreiber. New York: Associated American Artists, 1946.

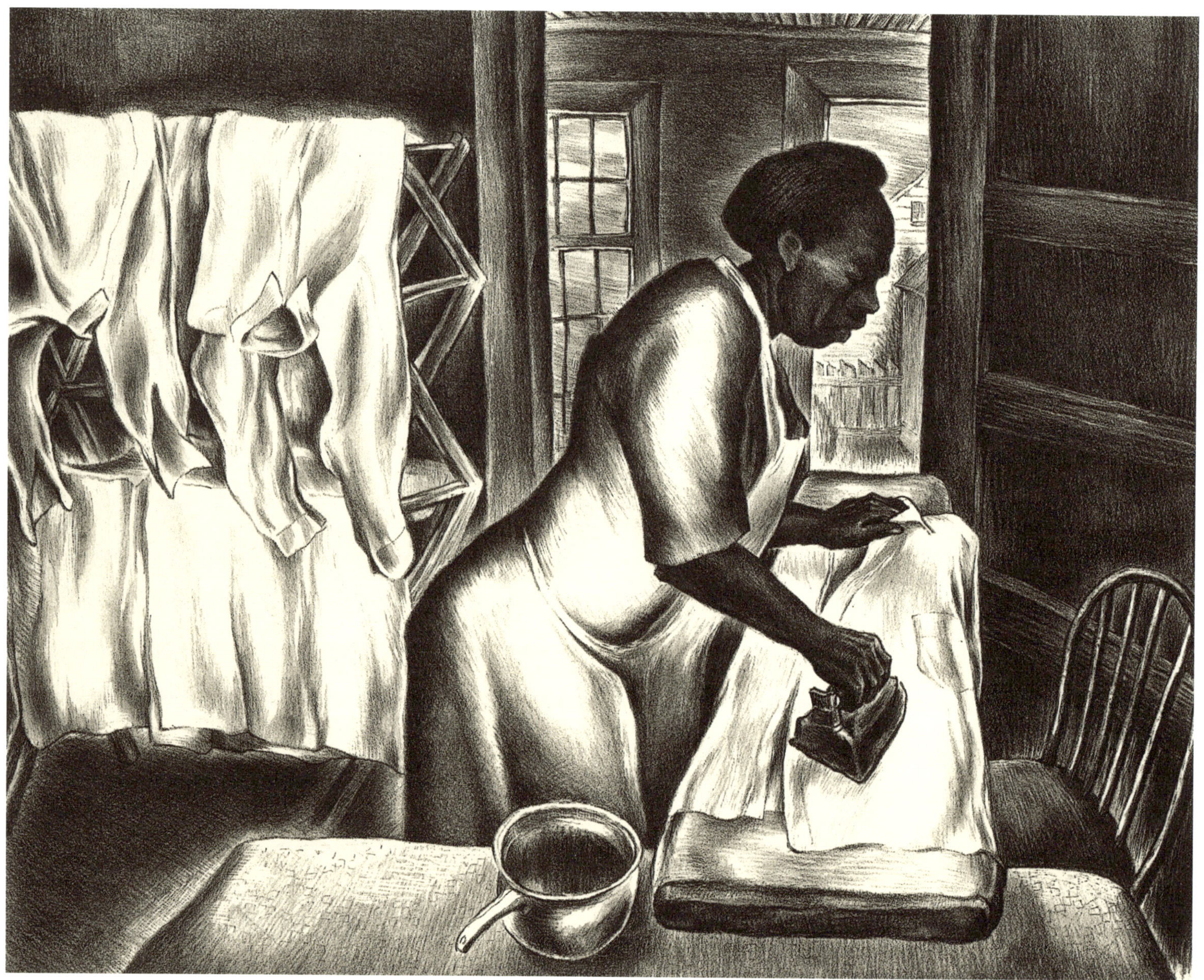

JOHN SLOAN, 1871-1951

Sloan grew up in Philadelphia, Pennsylvania, and attended high school with collector Albert Barnes and fellow artist William Glackens. He left school at age sixteen to work for a book and print dealer, where he became familiar with the work of Dürer and Rembrandt. In 1892 he joined the staff of the *Philadelphia Inquirer* as an illustrator and began to study at the Pennsylvania Academy of the Fine Arts. In 1904 he moved to New York where, as an independent artist painting scenes of city life, he helped organize The Eight show of 1908, along with Robert Henri and William Glackens. He then became active politically, joining the Socialist Party and running as a candidate for the New York State Assembly. In 1912, he joined the editorial staff of *The Masses* and helped revamp the journal, contributing regularly until his abrupt departure during the magazine's artists' strike in 1916. In the 1920s, secure as an independent artist, Sloan divided his time between New York City; Santa Fe, New Mexico; and Gloucester, Massachusetts.

Elzea, Rowland, and Elizabeth Hawkes. *John Sloan: Spectator of Life*. Philadelphia: University of Pennsylvania Press, 1988.

Loughery, John. *John Sloan: Painter and Rebel*. New York: Henry Holt and Company, 1995.

St. John, Bruce. *John Sloan*. New York: Praeger Publishers, 1971.

Zurier, Rebecca. *Art for the Masses: A Radical Magazine and Its Graphics, 1911-1917*. Philadelphia: Temple University Press, 1988.

Figure 38

MEYER WOLFE. *Tuesday—Othelia.*
Lithograph. 1934.

Meyer Wolfe created his first series of lithographs, called American Negro Life, in 1934 while employed by the Public Works of Art Project. In *Tuesday—Othelia* he depicts an African American woman, possibly a domestic servant or laundress, in the weekly activity of ironing clothing.

LAWRENCE BEALL SMITH, 1909-1995

Lawrence Beall Smith was born in Washington, D.C., studied at the Art Institute of Chicago, and received a bachelor of philosophy degree in 1931 from the University of Chicago. In the thirties and forties, Smith worked as a painter and lithographer, serving as an artist and war correspondent during World War II. Exploring diverse media, Smith began to sculpt in the 1960s, inspired by the indigenous rocks along the Maine coast where he spent his summers.

Lawrence Beall Smith. Bethlehem, Conn.: June 1 Gallery, [1985?].

Lawrence Beall Smith: Paintings and Lithographs, 1937-1951. New York: Susan Teller Gallery, 1993.

Salpeter, Harry. "About Laurence [*stet*] Smith." *Coronet* 6, no 5 (September 1939): 102-6.

MOSES SOYER, 1899-1974

The twin brothers Moses and Raphael Soyer were born near the Russian town of Borisogliebsk, but the family moved to the United States in 1912. Moses Soyer left high school to spend his adolescence working during the day and attending art classes at night. He chose to attend different classes from his brother, starting in 1916 at Cooper Union. He continued his studies at the National Academy of Design School of Art, in Robert Henri's class at the Ferrer Center, and, after winning a fellowship in 1926, through travels in Europe. Between 1927 and 1934 he taught art at several institutions, including the settlement house Educational Alliance School of Art and the New School for Social Research.

Kleeblatt, Norman L., and Susan Chevlowe, eds. *Painting a Place in America: Jewish Artists in New York, 1900-1945: A Tribute to the Educational Alliance Art School*. New York and Bloomington, Ind.: The Jewish Museum and Indiana University Press, 1991.

Moses Soyer: Oil Paintings and Works on Paper. Springfield, Ohio: Springfield Art Center, 1982.

Moses Soyer: Small Paintings. New York: ACA Galleries, 1977.

Social Art in America, 1930-1945. New York: ACA Galleries, 1981.

RAPHAEL SOYER, 1899-1987

Raphael Soyer, the twin brother of Moses, was born near the Russian town of Borisogliebsk and came to the United States in 1912. Like his brother, he quit high school and began attending art classes at night while working during the day.

Best known for his paintings, Raphael Soyer worked in the social realist style long after many other artists had abandoned it for modernism.

Cole, Sylvan, Jr. *Raphael Soyer: Fifty Years of Printmaking, 1917-1967.* New York: Da Capo Press, 1967.

Gettings, Frank. *Raphael Soyer: Sixty-five Years of Printmaking.* Washington: Smithsonian Institution Press, 1982.

Goodrich, Lloyd. *Raphael Soyer.* New York: Frederick A. Praeger, 1967.

Soyer, Raphael. "Résumé of an Aged Artist." *Art & Antiques,* January 1988, pp. 68-73, 104, 106.

Watson, Ernest W. "The Paintings of Raphael Soyer." *American Artist* 12 (June 1948):28-33.

BERNARD JOSEPH STEFFEN, 1907-1980

Bernard Steffen worked for the Resettlement Administration (1935-37) as staff artist, a position that required that he travel widely. He had studied at the Kansas Art Institute, at the Colorado Springs Art Center under Boardman Robinson, at the Los Angeles Art Institute, and at the Art Students League under Thomas Hart Benton. He worked mainly in lithography but also produced paintings and serigraphs.

Bernard Steffen. New York: Tasca Gallery, 1965.

"Contemporary Arts Presents Steffen, Kansan," *Art Digest,* October 1, 1937.

Francey, Mary. *Depression Printmakers as Workers: Re-Defining Traditional Interpretations.* Salt Lake City: Utah Museum of Fine Arts, University of Utah, 1988.

North, Bill, and Stephen H. Goddard. *Rural America: Prints from the Collection of Steven Schmidt,* p. 36. Lawrence: Spencer Museum of Art, University of Kansas, 1993.

Steffen, Bernard. Correspondence of the Region 2 Office (New York area) with artists, 1933-34, Records of the PWAP, Record Group 121, National Archives. Microfilm Reel DC 114. Archives of American Art, Washington, D.C.

———. Vertical file, National Museum of American Art/National Portrait Gallery Library, Smithsonian Institution, Washington, D.C.

HARRY STERNBERG, born 1904

Harry Sternberg, who grew up and attended high school on the Lower East Side in New York City, took classes at the Art Students League at night, while working during the day. In 1927 he began experimenting with soft ground, aquatint, drypoint, and line etching and in 1933 he became an instructor in etching, lithography, and composition at the Art Students League. A Guggenheim Foundation grant for the summer of 1936 allowed him to begin a series on the coal and steel industry. After living in New York for sixty years, Sternberg settled in Escondido, California, finding artistic inspiration from the desert there as he had from the streets of New York.

Acton, David. *A Spectrum of Innovation: Color in American Printmaking, 1890-1960.* New York: Norton, 1990.

Landau, Ellen G. *Artists for Victory: An Exhibition Catalog.* Washington: Library of Congress, 1983.

Moore, James C. *Harry Sternberg: A Catalog Raisonné of His Graphic Work.* Wichita, Kans.: Edwin A. Ulrich Museum of Art, Wichita State University, 1975.

Pohl, Frances K. *In the Eye of the Storm: An Art of Conscience, 1930-1970.* San Francisco: Pomegranate Artbooks, 1995.

Warner, Malcolm. *The Prints of Harry Sternberg.* San Diego: San Diego Museum of Art, 1994.

PRENTISS TAYLOR, 1907-1991

After studying lithography with Eugene Fitsch and Charles Locke of the Art Students League in New York in 1931, Prentiss Taylor returned to his hometown, Washington, D.C., in 1935, making lithographs of such local subjects as a storefront church near Union Station, as well as treating incidents of national interest such as the Scottsboro trial. He worked as an art therapist from 1943 through 1978 and lectured on painting at American University from 1955 to 1975.

Forty Years of Lithographs by Prentiss Taylor, 1931-1971. Washington: Franz Bader, 1971.

Rose, Ingrid, and Roderick S. Quiroz. *The Lithographs of Prentiss Taylor: A Catalogue Raisonné.* Bronx, N.Y.: Fordham University Press, 1996.

Welzenbach, Michael. "Starting with Diversity: Prentiss Taylor at Georgetown." *Washington Post,* September 15, 1990.

CHARLES WHITE, 1918-1979

When he joined the WPA Federal Art Project after completing studies at the Art Institute of Chicago, Charles White was able to explore twin themes that concerned him: racial prejudice and ignorance. Other artists in the program introduced him to both the ideas of Karl Marx and the work of Mexican muralists, who used historical subjects to educate people on social issues. In 1942, White left Chicago, his birthplace, to move to New York, where he studied at the Art Students League under Harry Sternberg, whose style greatly influenced his own. White preferred black-and-white drawing to working in other media, in part because of the ease of reproduction. In 1956 he moved to California to teach at the Otis Parson School of Design, work in film, and paint.

Alone in a Crowd: Prints of the 1930's-40's by African-American Artists: From the Collection of Reba and Dave Williams. 2nd rev. ed. New York: Washburn Press, 1993.

Killens, John Oliver. "Charles White: The People's Artist." *Georgia Review* 40, no. 2 (Summer 1986):449-72.

White, Frances Barrett, with Anne Scott. *Reaches of the Heart.* New York: Barricade Books, 1994.

ELIZABETH WHITE, 1893-1976

Elizabeth White was born, worked, and taught in Sumter, South Carolina, where she was one of the most well known artists in the state during the New Deal era. Although she remained in North and South Carolina for most of her life, White studied at the Pennsylvania Academy of the Fine Arts and spent summers at the MacDowell Colony in Peterborough, New Hampshire. She studied printmaking with Frank Tankwell in New York and Alfred Hutty in Charleston, had her own printing press, and pulled her own prints. She also painted and worked to foster the arts in South Carolina.

Haile, Priscilla (Director, Sumter Gallery of Art, Sumter, South Carolina). Communication with Sara Duke, August 18, 1998.

Phagan, Patricia, ed. *The American Scene and the South: Paintings and Works on Paper, 1930-1946.* Athens: Georgia Museum of Art, 1996.

MEYER WOLFE, 1897-1985

Born in Louisville, Kentucky, Wolfe grew up in Nashville, Tennessee, and studied in Chicago at the Academy of Fine Arts and then in New York at the Art Students League under John Sloan. In New York, Wolfe worked as a newspaper illustrator. In 1926 he went to Paris to train under Pierre Lauren at the Académie Julien. His work was exhibited at the New York World's Fair in 1939 and both his paintings and sculpture were widely shown after World War II.

Acarino, Nicole S. (Assistant Art Curator, Vanderbilt University Fine Arts Gallery, Nashville, Tennessee). Communication with Sara Duke, November 11, 1998.

Hieronymus, Clara. "Meyer Wolfe Returns 'Home' in Show." *The Tennessean* (Nashville), November 18, 1979.

Muessig, Laura (Acting Assistant Registrar, Weisman Art Museum, University of Minnesota, Minneapolis). Communication with Sara Duke, October 8, 1998.

Robertson, Bruce. *Representing America: The Ken Trevey Collection of American Realist Prints: University Art Museum, University of California, Santa Barbara.* Santa Barbara: University Art Museum, University of California; Seattle: Distributed by the University of Washington Press, 1995.

Seaton, Elizabeth G., (Ph.D. candidate, Northwestern University). Communication with Sara Duke, October 17, 1998.

Wolfe, Meyer. Correspondence of the Region 2 Office (New York area) with artists, 1933-34, Records of the PWAP, Record Group 121, National Archives. Microfilm Reel DC 114. Archives of American Art, Washington, D.C.

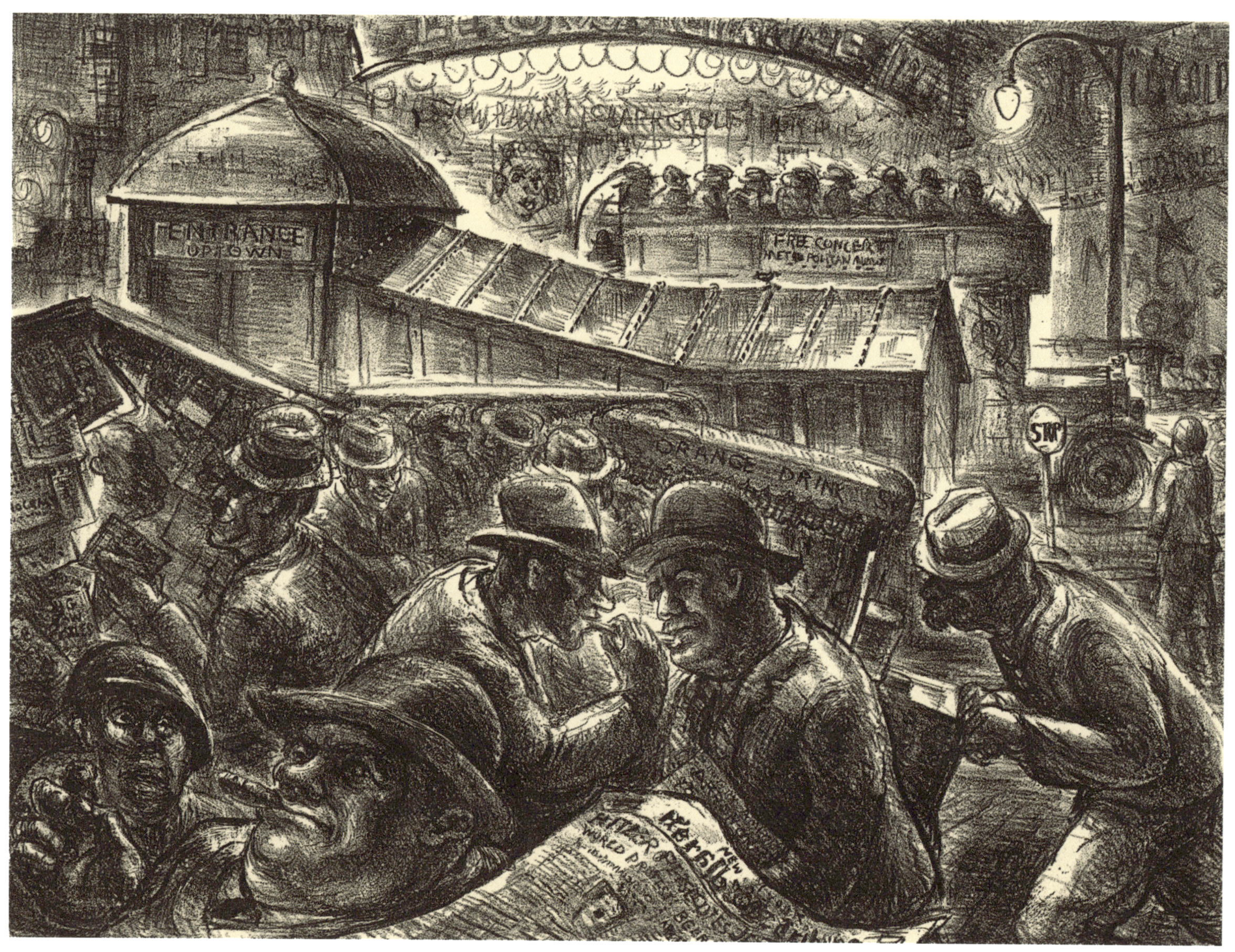
ENTRANCE
UPTOWN
FREE CONCERT
METROPOLITAN
ORANGE DRINK
STOP

Figure 39
JAMES PENNEY. *Columbus Circle.*
Lithograph. 1932.
Reproduction courtesy of
the Estate of James Penney.

James Penney was just twenty-two years old when he produced this dynamic view of the hustle and bustle surrounding Columbus Circle in New York City, which he created while studying lithography under Charles Locke at the Art Students League.

Alone in a Crowd: Prints of the 1930's-40's by African-American Artists; from the Collection of Reba and Dave Williams. 2nd rev. ed. New York: Washburn Press, 1993.

Art for All: American Print Publishing between the Wars. Washington: Smithsonian Institution Press, 1980.

Balk, Eugene. "The 'American Scene' Print and the Cartoon." *Print Quarterly* II, no. 4 (December 1994): 379-94.

Ekedal, Ellen, and Susan Barnes Robinson. *The Spirit of the City: American Urban Paintings, Prints, and Drawings, 1900-1952.* Los Angeles: Loyola Marymount University, 1986.

Francey, Mary. *Depression Printmakers as Workers: Re-Defining Traditional Interpretations.* Salt Lake City: Utah Museum of Fine Arts, University of Utah, 1988.

Graphic Excursions—American Prints in Black and White, 1900-1950: Selections from the Collection of Reba and Dave Williams. Essays by Karen F. Beall and David W. Kiehl. Boston: D.R. Godine in association with the American Federation of Arts, 1991.

Harrison, Helen A., and Lucy R. Lippard. *Women Artists of the New Deal Era: A Selection of Prints and Drawings.* Washington: National Museum of Women in the Arts, 1988.

Hills, Patricia. *Social Concern and Urban Realism: American Painting of the 1930s.* Boston: Boston University Art Gallery, 1983.

Landau, Ellen G. *Artists for Victory: An Exhibition Catalog.* Washington: Library of Congress, 1983.

Masteller, Richard Nevin. *We, the People? Satiric Prints of the 1930s.* Walla Walla, Wash.: Donald H. Sheehan Gallery, Whitman College, 1989.

Muller, Mary Lee. *Imagery of Dissent: Protest Art from the 1930s and 1960s.* Madison, Wis.: Elvehjem Museum of Art, University of Wisconsin-Madison, 1989.

North, Bill, and Stephen H. Goddard. *Rural America: Prints from the Collection of Steven Schmidt.* Lawrence: Spencer Museum of Art, University of Kansas, 1993.

O'Connor, Francis V., ed. *Art for the Millions: Essays from the 1930s by Artists and Administrators of the WPA Federal Art Project.* Greenwich, Conn.: New York Graphic Society, 1973.

Oles, James. *South of the Border: Mexico in the American Imagination, 1917-1947.* Trans. Marta Ferragut. Washington: Smithsonian Institution Press, 1993.

Park, Marlene, and Gerald E. Markowitz. *Democratic Vistas: Post Offices and Public Art in the New Deal.* Philadelphia: Temple University Press, 1984.

Phagan, Patricia, ed. *The American Scene and the South: Paintings and Works on Paper, 1930-1946.* Athens: Georgia Museum of Art, 1996.

Pohl, Frances K. *In the Eye of the Storm: An Art of Conscience, 1930-1970; Selections from the Collection of Philip J. and Suzanne Schiller.* San Francisco: Pomegranate Artbooks, 1995.

Williams, Lynne Barstis. *American Printmakers, 1880-1945: An Index to Reproductions and Biocritical Information.* Metuchen, N.J.: Scarecrow Press, 1993.

Williams, Reba, and Dave Williams. *American Screenprints.* New York: National Academy of Design, 1987.

Zurier, Rebecca. *Art for the Masses: A Radical Magazine and Its Graphics, 1911-1917.* Philadelphia: Temple University Press, 1988.

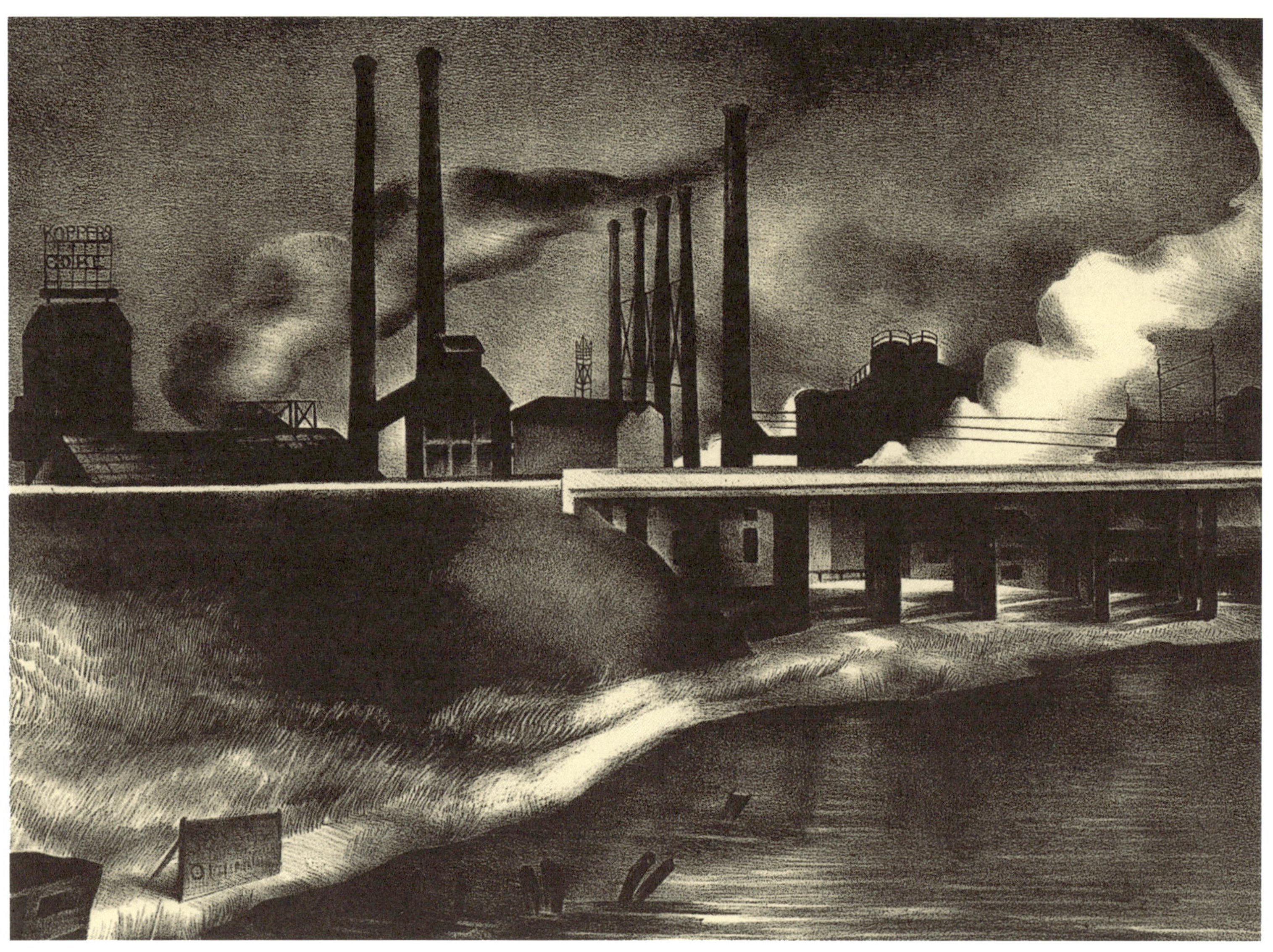

KOPPERS
COKE

Figure 40
VICTORIA HUTSON HUNTLEY.
Koppers Coke.
Lithograph. 1932.
Reproduction courtesy of Matteo Ledinic.

Victoria Hutson Huntley won first prize at the Philadelphia Print Club's National Exhibition in 1933 for *Koppers Coke.* Writing of the print two years later, she said, "It is difficult for me to gage [*sic*] accurately the exact time period necessary for me to complete a lithograph. Sometimes I spend days on a relatively small area—putting tone on tone in order to arrive at the richness of value and texture which I find necessary....I worked a week just on the sky of *Kopper's Coke* and that included nights as well."

Page references in ***bold italics*** refer to illustrations.

The text and captions for this book were set
in the Gill Sans family. The British designer
Eric Gill designed Gill Sans as a text face in
the late 1920s. The display type, Laser, is a
digital face designed by Martin Wait in 1987.
The text and illustrations were printed on
100 lb. Mohawk Superfine, eggshell finish; the
cover on 130 lb. Mohawk Superfine cover.
The endpapers are Rainbow Antique Charcoal. The book was printed and bound by
Steckel Printing, Inc., Lancaster, Pennsylvania.
The book was designed and composed by
Adrianne Onderdonk Dudden.